ROOTLING

Katie Donovan was born in 1962 and grew up on a farm in Co. Wexford, but for most of her life she has lived in Dun Laoghaire. She was educated at Trinity College Dublin and the University of California at Berkeley. She lived in Hungary for a year before returning to Ireland where she was a journalist with the *Irish Times* for 13 years. She qualified as an Amatsu practitioner (a form of Japanese osteopathy) and combines this work with teaching Creative Writing at IADT, the Institute of Art, Design and Technology in Dun Laoghaire.

Her latest book of poetry, *Rootling: New & Selected Poems* (Bloodaxe Books, 2010), draws on three previous collections, *Watermelon Man* (1993), *Entering the Mare* (1997) and *Day of the Dead* (2002), together with a whole collection of new work.

She is the author of *Irish Women Writers: Marginalised by Whom?* (Raven Arts Press, 1988), and has co-edited two anthologies, *Dublines* (with Brendan Kennelly), published by Bloodaxe Books in 1996, and *Ireland's Women: Writings Past and Present* (with A. Norman Jeffares and Brendan Kennelly), published by Kyle Cathie (Britain) and Gill and Macmillan (Ireland) in 1994.

KATIE DONOVAN

ROOTLING

NEW & SELECTED POEMS

Katie Donovan

BLOODAXE BOOKS

Copyright © Katie Donovan 1993, 1997, 2002, 2010

ISBN: 978 1 85224 881 9

First published 2010 by
Bloodaxe Books Ltd,
Highgreen,
Tarset,
Northumberland NE48 1RP.

www.bloodaxebooks.com
For further information about Bloodaxe titles
please visit our website or write to
the above address for a catalogue.

Supported by
**ARTS COUNCIL
ENGLAND**

Cover design: Neil Astley & Pamela Robertson-Pearce.

Printed in Great Britain by
Bell & Bain Limited, Glasgow, Scotland.

for my children
Phoebe and Felix

ACKNOWLEDGEMENTS

This book includes poems selected from three previous collections published by Bloodaxe Books: *Watermelon Man* (1993), *Entering the Mare* (1997) and *Day of the Dead* (2002). Acknowledgements are due to the editors of the following publications in which some of the new poems in *Rootling* first appeared: *The Irish Times, Poetry Ireland Review, An Sionnach, Tsunami* (TCD Press, 2005), *The Scaldy Detail 2007*, ed. Eamonn Wall (Scallta Media), *The Shop, Something beginning with P.*, ed. Seamus Cashman (O'Brien Press, 2004), and *Stand*.

I am indebted to the Arts Council of Ireland/An Chomhairle Ealaíon for Bursaries received in Literature in 2006 and 2009, which gave me time to work on the poems in *Rootling* and to shape the book as it now appears. Thanks are also due to Dun Laoghaire/Rathdown County Council and IADT, joint funders of the Writer-in-Residence post I held in 2006-08. Part of the residency involved working on the poems in *Rootling*.

Several all-too-short stays in the Tyrone Guthrie Centre at Annaghmakerrig helped with the evolution of *Rootling*. Thanks to all concerned.

Finally I would like to acknowledge the support of poet and friend Siobhán Campbell during two decades of poetry-writing.

CONTENTS

Rootling

(2010)

Bag of Cats

The smallest cat
purrs sleekest
because of you:
her butter man.
The fattest cat
spreads out
lugubrious,
and the princess
white cat
arches her prance
at your approach.

The night
my claws come out
the white one
climbs your shoulder,
snuggling your neck,
her yellow eyes
warning me
to cool it.

You've won them over –
the real custodians
of the house.

I held out
the longest
fearing my losses
as you moved in.

But now
when the wind
tears the night,
and the rain
bullies the trees:
all of us
want to burrow

into the heat
of your armpit.

Without you
we'd be a sorry
bag of cats.

Studying the Bones

You dance inside me
as you knit your bones.

I can feel
the round
of your skull,
as delicate
as a porcelain cup
in the curve
of my saucer.

As you swim within –
conductor of my heart,
wind of my breath,
gurgle of my waters –
I grapple
with the tough, unrotting
core of my past.
It piles into my dreams
and fills my house
with skeletons.

The smallest shells,
my brother, sisters –
their deathbuds
are a garland
for my living throat.

Each day
I find a dried up
souvenir.

Will I ever shed enough
to make your passage clear?

I dream of landslides,
bulldozers; wake to hurricanes
reshuffling the hours.

You are a candle
in the vault:

I will bear you out.

The Swimmers

Mushroom-bellied, we struggle into suits
and swivel to the pool.
Buoyed by water and heat,
by the exhortations of our coach,
we blossom into billowing ballerinas –
more than just the sum of our ranked pots.
Our naked arms describe great arcs;
our faces, framed in tight caps,
are dreamy, our legs twirling,
our loosening frames held
by liquid blue, our babies
riding the flow as we kick and glide,
puffing out of our shrunken lungs.

Four of us sway –
languid monsoon flowers –
in our last week before the deluge.
We are quiet; serious;
then laughing – nothing
seems quite right;
and when we haul
out of our ripply field,
into the rigmarole
of bras, trousers, lacing shoes,
we leave singly, bracing
into the night.

Alive

Straddled,
like a cow in a fair,
I shudder as the midwife
strips me bare,
and my waters gush
across the floor.

You see my bottom
flower like a baboon's
as I brace and grunt;
you're calm throughout,
and fascinated, as her head
breaks free, as she rests
on my belly in slimy red.

You are triumphant
when we take her home,
but I'm prone
to shakes and weeps,
hovering over the tiny
neckless scrap,
looking out for threats.

You throw her
over your shoulder,
laughing as you tell
of baby horrors:
the German newborn
chewed by the family dog,
the premature boy
boiled to death
in the hospital linen,

the day-old passenger
in the car
which crashed into a lake
drowning the parents
but the child –
immersed in cold water
for an hour –
emerged alive.

Rootling

Little wrestler,
you snort, snuffle
and lunge;
latching on
like a cat
snatching and worrying
her prey.
Once attached,
you drag on me
like a cigarette,
puffing between sucks,
nose pressed close,
somehow catching
your wheezy breath.
Between rounds,
in your white wrap
you arch your back
for a rub,
like I'm your coach,
readying you
for newfound strength
in the ring.
Your fists flail,
fingers hooking
my nursing bra,
your feet curl and kick,
toes a feast
of tiny action.
There is nothing romantic
in this vital ritual,
yet I crane over you,
a loose sack,
liquid with the loss
of your form,
with the tears of labour
and lolling hormones
making me gush
along with my womb,
still churning out afterbirth.

So when
you dandle my nipple
with a gummy smile,
I tell myself
your grin's for me,
even if you've got
that look
of a seasoned souse
on his most
delicious tipple.

Phoebe in the Bath on My 40th Birthday

Your big blue eyes are wide
as you slide down the mountainside
of my legs, as you plonk on my breasts,
seeing, suddenly, there are two –
you suck on both, just to be sure.
You frog-leg in the water,
squealing up a storm,
skin on my skin, like the morning
you were born.

Five months ago, I lay here,
a pool within a pool,
feeling your liquid manoeuvres
deep in my interior.
And now you're out –
grown long and bold, wriggling
with the urge to move, hold,
taste the world on your hard gum rim.

You love the water's heat and lift,
my minnow; swanlet,
you push me to the brink –
I'll grab back handfuls of myself,
some day, when you are launching out from me
into the vast sea, and the island body
where you played and fed and grew,
dwindles to the memory of a light that shone,
brightest for you, girl, always for you.

Carrying My Father Up the Stairs

When I see my baby's pate
with its straggly hairs,
and her ears – the right one
sticking out – I'm put in mind
of my father, the same ear
permanently cocked,
on the same side
of a balding head.
Then there's the lofty
vulnerable pose she assumes
while dozing, and
lately she has even started
his habit of chewing her tongue.
When I pick her up
on an evening
that finds me hazy with fatigue,
and carry her upstairs,
I could be lifting him.

I'll take his spirit with me,
his courage and his civic pride,
his caring more than a damn
about the bigger picture.
I'll leave his horsewhip of duty
at the foot of the stairs,
too often used
to stripe himself.
I'll drop his guilt
like an old wrap
the moths have eaten through.
Better to keep
his natty look, his ready laugh,
his tender way with animals.

I'll not bear his regrets –
it's hard enough to shed my own –
and I'll try to lose
his awkward hauteur,
though it sings around my head

like a swarm of flies,
getting between me
and the world's heat.

I'll never shed
the print of his loneliness,
how – caught between faultlines
of Irish, Scot, and 'good English schools' –
he could never be
the child of a tribe.

I lay my baby in her downy cot,
imagining my father, miles away,
tossing in his night-time sleeplessness,
his fine mind flayed with frets.
I wish the three of us –
root, branch and leaf –
harmony; protection; rest;
as I lurch, exhausted,
to my own bed.

Maiden Voyage

On her first trip
to the land of Grimm
how quickly her lips
bestow a smile
on the wartiest old lady,
lassoing the lined face
in a loop of joy.
Her hands fasten happily
on new playthings: beaky toucan,
blue crawling bug; furry bear book.
Her own language spools
from the pretty bud
of her yodelling mouth,
singing la, la, la,
with her one tooth peeping out.
Her hands and feet
are windmills in the thrilling gusts
of the world, twirling faster
with the way a twist
of feathered grass
fondles her fat cheek,
the give of a tissue
tearing in her fingers.
Her laugh tickles the ceiling
when she holds one end
of a silver string,
and I the other –
we play skip rope
with our toy umbilicus.

Other Mothers

You, with your powdered organic baby rice,
feeling weary as you squeeze
your tight breast for milk to mix the stuff,
recall our lives, half grown ourselves,
our milk sucked dry,
our bellies already filled with the next one,
we chewed on the hard portion of our daily fare
to break it down and smear their little mouths
with half our share. We had none
of what you have, and by your age,
most of us were dead, or left without
a single tooth in our head. Your calf
is twice the size of what we reared:
count yourself lucky she's alive.

And yes, although it was our open grave
that faced us, we still gave what we had
with all the fierce exhausted gladness
that you feel, falling slowly
from the peak of girlhood,
our flesh loose and hair gone grey,
barely able to run from predators,
yet doubly clinging to the young we made,
our cries too terrible
for any but the sharpest claws.
Some, like the bears
would spare us if we showed a breast
all leaky with sticky flow
you're trickling now.

And if we lived to grow too old
to hatch our own,
we carried those we could
for other mothers,
our hearts sore for the days
when they were ours,
kissing with our eager lips
the newborn skin,
the precious shining eyes.

When I Let You Fall

so many other things
fell too.
The statue of myself
as perfect mother
was first to hit the floor.
My plate of perfect plans –
like puff pastries
full of air –
flew from my hand.
My rod of blame
came down upon me
with such a whack
it broke.

You sit before me
in your rakish hat
full of glee:
no memory
of my treachery.

Your smile says:
Lift me up, mother,
in hands I trust.

Holiday Morning

(for Jon and Bev)

You lollop to the glass and pull up,
hands splayed and eyes fastened
on the wonders of your holiday garden:
squirrels skittering, cardinals fluttering,
a humming-bird lifting a tiny beak to feed.

Watching the tail-twitching, nut-nibbling,
belly-crawling goings-on, your mouth
forms an 'o' that your voice speaks;
finger-pointing, you attempt a new word,
and when 'squirrel' proves elusive,
you purr 'bird'. In your timbre
it sounds like an avian call,
and it's true you live more nearly
in their world, so moved are you
by grass and flowers, the alert-eared dogs,
the fling of the branch-leaping squirrels,
each flight and tumble the morning yields.

Fowl Play

(for Sharon and Philip)

The red-combed cock,
with his glistening green tail
and sturdy, long-nailed claws,
shakes his wattles and perts his head,
darting; viewing you side-to-side.

You stand enthralled,
no taller than this loud-throated strutter,
your little toes bare
in your first summer sandals,
your tummy pooching out
as you stare and stare.

His scaly legs bring him fast
into bushes, followed by the harem
of his five hens, clucking,
waggling, haggling, jerking,
nodding and fluffing, wondering
what to do with this bald intruder.

You stoop to consider
a lone hen in a cage – she swoops
over two leggy chicks,
fussing and pecking
to send you away.

There's chickenshit on your soles
and down floating round your head,
my small inquisitive angel,
as you pursue the cock
and his procession of wives,
in and out of the roses,
until they retreat to the mucky shed
of their home, peering out crossly,
waiting in vain for you to give up.

Not for you the ball or trampoline,
the thin charm of toys,
this other life draws you
to try it on like a second skin.

The Lemurs

(for Jill and Jenny)

In her blue dress Phoebe sits,
dappled with green light,
fingers turning a yellow leaf.
Ring-tailed lemurs, tame and free
run beside her on the dusty path.
With black snouts and clever eyes,
they fling and swing, or sit like yogis
in patches where the sun beams heat,
opening their white bellies to June.

Females nurse their young
at little leathery breasts;
when dishes of cut fruit are served
babies ride on mother's back,
as, tail high, she speeds to feed.

The woodland park has other charms:
flamingoes in the shallows,
brown goats shading in the meadow,
deer above us in the long grass.

But Phoebe, once ensconsed,
prefers to linger here
with the lemurs in their busy grove,
where small digits frisk
our strollers and our baskets –
they quickly sniff the human picnic
once their own meal is devoured.

We shoo and laugh,
and almost capture one
to smuggle home.

Repose

I walk into the dim room where you sleep,
there is no repose quite like it:
you, snuggled and flushed in your lamb coverlet,
cuddled up with a lacy comforter,
a stuffed hare and a fluffy puppet pig.

The nightlight throws an amber glow
over a floor spread with pillows you arrayed,
laying a tired toy on each:
the enormous bunny in his silk bow tie,
the white mouse in her blue PJs; and the zebra,
with his half-lidded eyes and fascinating tail.

In among the slumber snores the fat black cat,
tucked in her bed beside the heat,
swathed like all the toys in her own blanket.

Come morning you will wake with friends,
rested and impatient for fresh sorties
up and down the stairs. You will object
unless at least three creatures are carried in your arms,
anxious they might miss the next event.

Till then my night will hum
with your gentle breath.

Cows

She has fallen in love with cows:
their huge, mild bodies
that chew and stare,
the way they stand
with lowered, curious heads
beside their fuzzy young,
or lie, lazing on their haunches
in the sun.

She makes her way on tiny legs,
close as she dares,
she points her little fist,
lowing luxuriantly with pursed lips:
'Moo.' Then waits
for them to say it too.

She can spot them fields away,
forms of rust or black and white,
just seeing them
is immense joy guaranteed,
visual satiation, the answering
of a patent need.

The creatures barely heed
their worshipper: small bald witness
of their horned beauty.
They sway, munching and blowing,
twitching and lifting their tails
to emit
fascinating streams of stink.

When the summer heat
cools to evening,
they lose their torpor,
and out of the curvaceous caverns
of their grass-filled bellies
come bellows and roars
leaving her aghast and thrilled.

They bawl for the farmer
and his cheeky dog
to take them in,
relieve the swollen lactic sacs
of their creamy load.

After milking, she ignores
the sunset's pinkening shawl,
to rush for one last look,
her hands pulling up
on the low stone wall;
the languid hulks –
like statues in the trodden grass –
remain insensible
to her urgent bed-time call,
to her radiant bliss
that they are there at all.

The Things I Do for You

Girl, I am stretched beyond myself
like a tree that is bent so far in a sea wind
it is almost drowned.
The gate I close on my private garden
only you, with your deft hands can open,
tear off its hinges and force me to gladness.
I have surrendered to you
like a foot soldier to a duke,
when in the parallel story
of my childless life, I am implacable.
You took my haughty face
to use upon me, a mocking weapon –
though not as potent
as your winning laugh and clever quest
that daily strikes new keys
to mark the opening of a song,
lifting me beyond the flattening of fatigue,
the tangled house; stink of the nappies
you already scorn to wear, so to fit you out
is a visoring for full confrontation.
Then there is the miraculous day
when you can tell in words and signs
what you've just done: a poo.

Bearing you
has been a devastation, and yet
the razing down of all my ordered plots
has somehow raised me up.

Tall

(for Phoebe, aged 20 months)

Scuffling up russet leaves
with small red shoes,
she relishes our walking routine,
where the tortoiseshell puss
hides and pounces
in autumn colours,
and she copies the way
I call the cat's name:
Titi, Titi.

She likes to go under trees
to reach for juicy berries,
to run downhill, to run riot
in the neighbours' gardens,
greeting dogs and wooden hedgehogs;

filling her fists with stones,
pine needles and cones,
testing the strength in her legs
as she climbs steps alone,
waiting for notice and praise.

She plays with my hair
in her fairy fingers,
as I shoulder her home,
under a speckled pink sky,
listening for the meow
of the waiting cat
as we approach our gate:

her mother is the giant
who makes fire,
who brings books alive,
who grows tall in the love
of her growing child.

11 Week Scan

At 41 I'm supposed to be too old
for the comfort of expecting
a normal child. As if playing
on my doubts, you send
leaks of blood, like a threat to leave
unless I cover you
in the splendid shower
of love and certainty you so deserve.
When I think I may have lost your hold
I am bitter like a fruit
afraid of winter, but later
the shop-bought test
tells otherwise – you've deigned
to stay, and soon your flipper limbs
lead my stomach
in a seasick waltz;
you suck me clean
though a carnival straw.

Still, riven with fears,
and feeling like a criminal,
I go for the early scan.
The cold ultrasound snout
offers glimpses of you,
my jumping bean,
and the nurse is pleased
with her measuring –
so much depends
on the contours
of your nuchal fold;
so much is left unsaid –
at last I am released.

You've won.

Let us fasten and fatten
as the weeks progress, let me find
new chambers in myself
and grow fuller than I ever dreamed.
My inner acrobat, now I'll grin,
heavy and greedy,
waiting for your outward swing.

Surfeit

I'd forgotten the day of the blues,
rinsing the birth triumph
as the breasts swell with milk
and the eyes with tears.
Here it is again, that day
piled with a surfeit of indignities:
pain, fatigue, feeling a failure
because the baby cannot feed.
I give myself to sorrow,
and fury that I must be seen
every fretting second
as a calm Madonna,
satiated with ecstasy.

It's no time since the birth
split me like a rocket,
as I hung bracing and cursing
on the edge of the bed,
and swung him, a winkled,
cone-headed gift,
into my shuddering hold.

So while my mother
counts my blessings,
I surrender to self-pity,
no room left for bravery
or brute push. Just
a wobbly, upset, fearful day;
pedestrian, when the miracle
is eclipsed by petty setbacks
riding mocking on a pair
of broken shoulders.

Tomorrow, not for anyone but him –
my smallest, newest love –
I will banish wan
and gather all my vim,
but, for now, this is waste ground,
and I am puling at the water's rim.

The Boy

(for Felix)

Mizzling is his missile into my head:
it lands and cracks me open,
I can't think or do a thing until he stops.
As soon as I scoop his warm fleshy form
into the fit of mine, he is content,
flashing me his flirty grin,
turning his pretty head to watch
whatever his eye can catch.
He trails his hand in the sink's warm suds,
pulling out a wooden spoon; next,
he grabs the towel rail, marvelling
at the smooth pole twisting in his hands,
pulling on it like a grown boy
testing a bar's potential swing.
He snuggles to my neck,
fingers reaching down to anchor mine.
Thus held he would be sanguine
in the face of a maniac or hissing snake.

I am his warm home hammock;
his viewing tower; his lunch;
his cosying dawdle; his work-out station;
his toting and doting slave.
I bear him like an elephant
carrying a brahmin potentate,
I suffer him to bite and and smite
the nipple that feeds him,
I give him my finger to gnaw
like a puppy worrying a shoe.

I wipe each pouch and crevice
free of the mustard poo he oozes,
I let his little feet
beat on my belly like a drum,
his weight hang from a grip of my hair.

He is my wily explorer,
my charming conqueror –
who would have thought
I would finally submit?

Sleep

Come to me, best companion,
for you I'll lose the teasing muses,
the brain's ceaseless surgical analysis,
what I crave is not lust, nor even tenderness,
but long hours of oblivion.
A selfish lone float of recuperation,
without interruption (not even to pee or feed)
would be infinite bliss indeed.
After this embrace – that only you can give –
I'll wake with my face reshaped
into a pleasing semblance of my youth,
my eyes without their veins of red,
my joints oiled and gliding as they should.
Just raise your mantle
over my worn out body and I will breathe
as cosy and silent as a daisy,
all my petals folded, waiting
for enough sun to convince me it is day.

Tea Shop

I needn't have sought to win her back
with ice cream and cake in the tea shop,
'Pinocchio' secured for her delectation, later.
What she liked was our sojourn down the hill,
through the thicket where normally we can't go
with the baby in his bulky buggy.
She said hello to the fish and birds
swivelling and tweetering in the pet shop,
and the bakery could be borne in spite
of the lady with 'a spiderweb on her face'.
Now we sit quietly, me marvelling
at how big she is, it seems a blink
since she was bald and new.
She's had to grow up faster than she'd like
since he appeared, the little brother
who so often now monopolises my arms.

Keeping her fist wrapped tight
around her yellow lolly, she moves
like a gliding snail from her chair
to my knee, and curls up cosily,
flushed and folded. This
is what she has been craving
for eight long months, what she's not
been having enough of. Lap time,
pressed–close–to–Mommy time –
nothing fancy, just the heat and comfort.
She nibbles the last of my cake
and tongues the cream off the plate.
All the while she is soaking up
a big fleshy Mommy embrace,
her cells storing it for later, for home,
when her brother fastens on my breast,
when the 6 P.M. crash comes,
and we regard each other crankily,
as I clatter with pots, dodge hungry cats,
keep an eye on the baby
and negotiate with her over TV.

Tia

The panda orange face
of my lithe, summer-loving cat
is sunk now, almost to her breast.
In days she's shrunk
from a slender thing
to stark starvation.
She's been with me some dozen years:
a proud, contrary grace,
a tree lover, bird plunderer,
a girl whose taste was for the high view,
sitting in solitary state at windows,
keeping guard on her place.
It was me she liked, not her plump
annoying daughters, nor my human child.
She pined when my affections
diverted and diluted,
yet when I could,
I'd cuddle her wiry limbs,
butt her flame-tipped head,
and from her lifted throat
she'd make her greeting song.

A prancer, light on her little pads,
she was always happy to stay out prowling;
but now when she keeps her distance
until dawn, I know she's insulted
by the useless surgery,
seeking cool undergrowth to relieve
the buzzing itch of her scar.
Next day she's lost a precious share
of dwindling strength. I weep
as I imprison her tonight, and check on her,
too late, my first babe, in wee hours,
finding her sitting stiff and sore,
scarcely able to drink, waiting
until she can taste the air again.

Antarctic Expeditions

He tries to interest me
in talk of Shackleton and Crean,
but I'm capsized
in the nausea of exhaustion
after another day
of small ones crying,
fighting, cajoling, hanging
their weights on me as though
I were some immortal tree.
They sleep now,
laced in a tangle of sweet features
and long lashes, while I slope around
sorting out the mayhem
of abandoned games,
and eat a too-late meal.
I can barely raise my chin
to be a dinner companion,
so close I am to cutting loose
and letting the whole lot of them sink.

Slowly he reels me in
with stories of failed expeditions,
all marked by bravery and stamina
and threats to very breath.
Shackleton died the day before
setting out again to the scene
of previous failure,
undaunted, aged 47.
And so I rouse myself, make one more
attempt to get to where we want –
I clean up, he fixes the broken video –
tomorrow we may not manage
to raise a flag, but we'll have put
our middle-aged determination
to work against the freeze,
so if nothing else, the joints
of this lumbering configuration
that is our family, don't seize.

Bedtime

My son, unable to sleep,
slithers all over me,
little thighs warm on my tummy,
he pets me possessively,
empties each breast
with practised ease.
I tell him about the night
when he was restless
to be born, how I sat
for hours with his sister,
listening to the rain,
watching dancing hippos
in *Fantasia*.
He sucks his thumb, bright-eyed
in the moonlit shadows
of the room.
His chat is all of diggers,
a man with a hat on,
falling down – poor man –
and how he will one day
have a beard upon his chin.
His sister snores beside us,
and finally his breathing
gets caught in the same rhythm,
as he surrenders – spreadeagled –
a tiny force-field
in the centre of the family bed.

Wildlife

I notice now that mother animals on TV
often look hassled and scrawny,
taking a swipe at their adorable,
photogenic cubs, in pure
exhausted irritation
(meanwhile the male sleeps on).
Then there's precious footage
where all play and fall
into the golden net of silliness,
the little furry ones jubilant,
the mother letting herself forget
about predators, hunger, parasites,
finding a dry bed for the night.
Usually this playful scene
is so treasured because it lasts
but minutes, before the mother
shakes herself and sets to,
licking out an infant ear.

I'm with you sister, as I compare myself
to nothing more than human duster,
I may not have to hunt my food
but I've to lug my squalling young
through parking lots and supermarkets,
I'm watchful too for danger,
not to mention being cook and waitress
when it comes to dinner.

Later it's time for wrestling and bared teeth,
my belly a trampoline, my feet and legs
fair game for leverage,
my strung-out arms their wings.

What My Hands Touch

Every day: drool, excrement,
nose snorts, spurts of sick.
The vast gushing of water
needed to clean up.
Wondering how the women cope
who have no tap.

Every day: baby skin, cat fur,
stale bedding, rumpled hair.
The vast gushing of water
needed to clean up.
Wondering how the women cope
who have no tap.

Every day: my own brittling skin,
veiny legs, nails that grow too long.
The vast gushing of water
needed to clean up.
Wondering how the women cope
who have no tap.

Every day: crinkle of old leaves,
clouts of earth, errant roots and weeds.
The vast gushing of water
needed to clean up.
Wondering how the women cope
who have no tap.

Every day: greasy plates and bowls,
tacky floors and toilet smells.
The vast gushing of water
needed to clean up.
Wondering how the women cope
who have no tap.

Wondering how the world
would turn if all those women
could turn the water on
just as easily as I do.

Only the desert
would be left.
A clean, lifeless vista,
of endless grains
of polished sand.

She Is Three

Blackberries, freshly plucked, are made for her mouth,
as are the corncobs, ripening their sweet kernels
in anticipation of her teeth. Her skin sips the August sun –
it tans her milk legs gold. She lollops in the dunes,
ladybirds crawling in her palm, oblivious
to tough sea plants scraping her nakedness,
then crawls to the water, plump girl bottom aloft,
offers her toes to the sleepy tongue of a wave,
flops in the shallows like a seal. In her net
she scoops pink-globed tentacles,
grabs the salty jellies in her bare hands
to fling them flat on the dry sand.

The meadow is for sprinting, her shoulders lifted,
creamy chin thrust out to greet the wind.
Trees plunk gnarled apples at her feet, she saves them,
balled in her skirt, for the soft-nosed shore horses.

At twilight, she longs over a yard full of drowsy hens,
tames a hungry black kitten all the way home.
Before settling she must first thrust her head
into a sky alight with stars, beside a tree dripping with plums.
She sleeps, cosy in her slanted attic room, dreaming
of fat spiders webbing each window of the house,
her round cheeks flushed, her arms outflung.

The Wave

(i.m. Robert Holohan and the victims of the Tsunami)

Amazing, how, the day after
a boy's body has been found –
dumped, despoiled – I see a mother wave,
as she sends her son alone into a shop
while she stays waiting in her car.
It is a triumph of belief
that, just for now, the flood
will not tear up the texture
of her very self: rend her boy away.

We need to nest so tightly
in our cosy wrap of knowing
that the tide will not swamp us today;
that the child will skip safely
from trawling predators
lurking inside a busy shop,
from trucks that hurtle
on the intervening road –
from the worst disasters the mind can picture –
to the open door of his mother's trust.

The Missing

Wand in hand,
my daughter casts a travelling spell
to keep me safe.
Pink feather wings and a silver crown
adorn her serious form,
as she grants me talismans –
a pretty drawing; a sweetie for the bus;
daisies in my pocket; and her speciality –
a big firm four-year-old hug.

When I arrive, I give the daisies water,
then unpack my picture.
Her fairies and ponies swim in a blue space,
with thoughtful blanks left for my words.

Birds and trees beckon
from my borrowed garden,
while I lie, flabbergasted in my empty room,
expecting any moment
her brother and herself to bounce in.

I hope a flight of poems will land
like the glimmer of swans
as they glide across the waiting lake,
instead at night a bat gets trapped
in my attic space, whirling in loops
of sinister horror when I wake.

If my girl were here, we'd laugh,
and tell each other the story of the bat,
she would draw him with his webby wings
and mouse's body, make of him
a cartoon thing.

After he's chased out,
I sit up, too rattled
to sleep in the strange bed,
realising how the missing
goes both ways,
wishing I could lay my head
beside her gently breathing face.

Island Pieces

(PEI, Canada, 2006)

I

Rain pellets the windows,
thunder grumbles at the soft red cliffs,
lightning takes its grim flash photos
of the swollen sky.

II

Corpses are washed up here,
hence the helicopters,
like dragonflies slicing the clouds,
seeking the unspeakable, inevitable return
of the castaway, and his small souvenirs.

III

A boat leaves harbour with hook and line,
stays out hours, chugging home in triumph,
to haul aloft the quarry –
a blue, glittering giant,
towed miles to shore
by a small crew of island men.
After a short display,
they hack the tuna –
its innards spill magenta
on the concrete waterfront –
my daughter, entranced,
elbows closer to the kill.

IV

Among the ochre of flat rocks
and green garlanding weed
are tide pools where she sits,
lost in games of winkles and wrack,
a pale nymph
in the layering of salt and sky,
surrounded by pink sand
that knows no desecration
of plastic bags or cans, just a trail
of crustacean bones where the birds
drop their dinners on the hard stones.

Resoling the Red Shoes

Red shoes with squared-off toes,
and a mary jane strap,
I wore them at a wedding, aged seven.
The sunny, cake-filled afternoon
sped by, me with one eye
firmly on my feet, shod for glory.
Too good for everyday,
they were adored, but rarely worn.
Soon I realised with horror
they were too small.
For years I dreamed
they'd fit my daughter.
Meanwhile they served as dress-up
for the girls of visitors,
who tried them on, coveting.
I felt selfish, like fate
would cheat me for my hoarding.
I almost buckled, deciding
I would never have the luck
of giving birth, so why not
pass them on? It was then
my daughter came, as if
to stake her claim.

At three she flopped
her shiny purloined booty
all over the noisy boards
of our house. Within a day
the soles were hanging off: old glue
worn thin with inactivity.
The shoes went to the cobbler,
who agreed to do a make-over
on thirty-five-year old patent leather.

Now she's six,
I think they'll finally fit.
Breath held, I invite her
to extend her toes,
expecting a Cinderella thrill.

Instead she wails:
they pinch; the strap hurts.
I sit back on my heels, mystified.
She runs off, barefoot.

Corner-facing

(for Wanda)

The time of reckoning comes
for my white cat:
after three months of struggle,
her body reaches its moment
where all my ploys are vain.
Her heart races and her breath is rank.

Outside this cold January night,
a vixen is pursued
by a balletic swain,
two leaping red-brushed lovers
cross my garden like
a bizarre apparition.

Inside I comb and pet,
offer morsels, feel
the closing of the room
around us, the chopping down
of space, like the last
of the dried up festive tree.

I place my hand
on the soft, elegant coat –
marked in cinnamon and grey –
it still deceives
with hints of remaining health.
She turns her pretty head
to the corner, and I tread
heavily up the stairs –
a lonely journey, the first of many
where she will not lead the way,
her bright whiskers peeking through
the banisters, ready for play.

Tree

I am out in the wind
and standing firm.

It's not like
being taken in
and showered
in silver.

Not like
being dressed in light,
my scent
lifting the room.

This is where
I don't have
to cut off
my roots.

Buying a Body

I would go to the mall
in my white rental car
and shop for a new heart for you,
father; choose lungs,
as strong and light
as parachutes.
I would purchase
the finest pair of wrists,
the fastest feet,
and legs as fleet
as a stag's.
I would go
to the sleep dispenser
and find you dreams
blue and serene
as your favourite summer sky.
I'd buy you time.
But I'm home
from the land of malls,
and I've turned in
the rental car.
It's just you and me
in the cold Sunday afternoon,
you gasping as the lamb
you thought your hands could hold
slips free; the mother bleating,
me not moving as quick
as you'd like
to shut the gate.

You urge me up the yard
the lamb's black legs
in my fist, and I wonder
why it takes so long for you
to follow.
I learn later
you're hardly able to walk it now,
but today you aimed
to pull the wool
over my eyes.

The Plan

I had my plan for when
I was going to get a hold of him –
the contrary mercurial old bull –
and tame him.
I knew eventually
his muscular machinations
would be stopped by a stroke,
and he'd be left half alive,
needing ministrations.
Those were to be the days
I'd pin him down,
tell him things,
hold the huge splay of his hand.

Those were the days
he'd have hated the worst,
being pushed around and cossetted.
So he took himself off pretty quick,
went out to cut the grass
one leaden afternoon,
and that was it.

I didn't even manage
to see him go, to have the comfort
of a bedside farewell.
I caught only the faint leap
of his blood – a fugitive heat –
still swimming upwards
like an unstoppable salmon
that barely falters even
as it falls.

Quietly

Quietly his last breaths were taken,
amidst the hospital fuss,
his wife knew he was sinking
beyond her grasp, even as
she argued with the matron
about tomorrow's tests.
Never one for silence
all his long life – the big laugh,
the noisy tread – his presence
shored us up on a swell of sound.
So quickly his breath dwindled
and he was still, the jaw down,
letting out the last exhale;
unbelievable in all his restless frame,
this moulded soundlessness,
this surrender.

Handing On

Here are your hands –
one a strong expanse,
little finger farthest out
(a spread my infant son
now sports, on the same hand –
the left); the other
a hard-worked tool,
the skin on its back
stained a deep blue,
gnarled and elongated
from clutching your stick
and taking your walking weight.
As you lie, quiet,
the heat almost sapped
from your frame,
your face already gaunt
and unfamiliar,
it is your hands I want to see,
to hold and remember,
their long work
finally over, the powerful
shapeshifters that always –
even as your body
brittled in age – seemed
sophisticated and able.
I rushed in vain to be here
for your last breaths,
and now I nurse the comfort
of your slim fingers and potter's thumb.
I wish my son a measure
of your strength, to test his mettle
at works like yours,
and hand them on.

The Dead House

In the house: silence.
The first morning it breathes
without his lungs.
A heavy morning,
the horse lies down in the field
with the weight of it.
The throats of the rooks
in the old trees are muted.
Morning here,
but no animating spirit
to rouse himself
and rotivate the rest.
The slugabeds,
they had no chance
when his voice called 'rise',
his stick pounding
the rhythm of getting going –
he couldn't stand
a wasted moment.

'Courage, mon vieu,' he'd say
in tears, each birthday,
amazed the length allotted him
his father and grandfather
taken in their prime, and he,
worn thin with many pains.

Now it's finished.
The quick heart
that pumped itself
into the centre of this place,
and was its engine,
has collapsed. The business done.
The long grass tamed.
The children grown
and partnered off.
The one son in place
to continue on, the others
in their stride.

And in the vast silence
of the first morning without him,
we lie like blasted skittles,
numb, unable to move
our arms and legs.

Limb

(for Richard and Christopher Donovan)

Severed from home –
which was divided anyway –
you were taken to the surgeon
and your leg removed.
Aged twelve, a highland dancer,
pony-rider, fleet and happy
in the breeze. A swimmer, climber,
showing the little ones
how things were done.

Your brother was kept in ignorance
until the last of what was going on:
the cutting of your limb.
He tried to run and stop
the grisly operation,
howling down the hospital walls.

You whiled away the days
in laughing at yourself
as you learned to get around
in the clumsy chair; later
the stumpy crutches;
finally, a false leg, made of tin.

When you died, your brother wept
not simply for the hero
he had looked up to all the years,
but for that boy,
taken down dark corridors,
his bright face; the waiting knife.

The Sleepy Unready Self

How I savoured, quietly, with tea
the hush of the house,
the gathering of myself
to meet the coming hours,
as my labouring began.

How few the moments
in the dark kitchen
before the crystallising of the pain,
the lugging of bags,
the bumpy car, frantic rapping
on the hospital door.
So soon the light came,
the huge heave and the child,
and all the world to share.

Death came that way too,
moving through the night,
the first call hardly pierced my ease –
it took some time for the cells
to begin their freeze; accept even
the possibility of loss. The next call came,
and still it was all slow, private,
with the same disbelief that
the threshold had finally appeared.

The sleepy, unready self must rise,
pack, drive, awkward in the bald spotlight
of the hospital, and all suddenly so public,
the metamorphosed fact of the corpse,
a parent transformed; startling
as the baby's compact push forth.

The quick night drains into day,
into flowers and people and explanations,
into public acts of demarcation,
phone calls, and friends and arrangements,
resting-places, clothes, and ceremonies;
what to put in the papers.

So little time to meditate
on familiar features, stilled,
on a whole new living child;
to touch a hand, kiss a brow;
say goodbye; say hello.

After

(for my mother)

Even after leaving him
she chose to continue
the long grafting of herself
to the land of his inheritance.

It was only years later,
when he died,
that she began to slip
into the swim
of who she once was:
a Canadian girl,
paddling a canoe,
with her sister in the back,
listening to the cries of loons.

After his funeral,
where she laid not him
but her youth
in a foreign grave,
where the vivid decade
of their life there
was already moss,
the bones of their lost babies,
dust – it was good to go home,
eat corn, feel the silk of lake water
welcome her skin,
hear voices like her own.

Tutu

My mother resurrects
the ballet dress she made for me:
white lily leaves over blue net.
It's torn and wrinkled
yet my daughter wants to wear it;
agrees, intrigued, to dig out
the faded black and white portrait
of me, her age – startlingly
the same, a dancer on the farm,
a polo stuffed under
the pearly satin bodice:
no central heating
in that freezing house.
I watch her now,
pirouette and preen,
accompanied by her brother,
doing his 'funky thing',
their arms sweep time
until I could be five again,
or three, my eyes turned in
to the dancer's reverie,
closed to the mysterious,
stiff adult interchange.

The dress was donned,
the leg stretched up, just so;
the fingers in their element,
like butterflies, so delicate,
the head inclined,
waiting and serene
to bear its jewelled crown;
one regal flourish
and then whoosh!
out of the room.

The Pins

The flat pitted head of the doll
was empty of his pink and green pins
and torn off his dimpled stump.
Her hands made disjointed moves
towards the littered floor.
Her room was growing cold and strange,
choked up with the broken toys
she had been told to put away.
They could not come along
to the new house – far off
in the city, and much smaller.
Her father would not come either.
He'd stay here alone,
and she would be his visitor.

Her crying soaked
the worn biscuit carpet:
tears for the lost parts
that would never be glued,
the hours where this room
had been her refuge.
Downstairs was dodgy always:
a marsh of teeth and cries.
Lately it was a place
where treachery began:
where she had found
her mother kissing another man.

Pink and green pins impale her skin,
useless, without a head to fit in.

Waking in Scotland

Waking in Scotland, it was always early:
sun long up, mountain heathers rolled out,
swans gliding across the lake,
anticipating bread from my hand.

Everyone was asleep, except her –
the small, fascinatingly wrinkled
and utterly powerful Scots granny,
who called my father 'boysie' –
and he a huge grown man.

Kind to me, she made her bed
a nest for two, for feasting from her tray
of tea and buttered toast.
We looked at books, she reading slowly
in her high crackly voice, me amazed
by her swollen arthritic fingers,
and the sudden hectic laugh.

That was our time –
later I'd be rowing on the lake;
she wielding secateurs in the garden;
walking the curly ginger dog;
or pontificating to the adults,
sitting like an elf in an armchair,
surveying her realm.

As I got older I began
to understand her better:
her father's beloved girl,
disinherited for a feckless brother,
she festered, her clever brain
pecking at crumbs,
when she was born to be a tycoon.

She nipped me harshly as I grew,
trying to prune me down to size,
and I still smart sometimes
from her stinging legacy.

But what stays more vividly –
especially this early summer day,
as I eat brown toast at home in bed,
eyeing a book – is our first ritual:
the mouse story she read me;
how good her breakfast tasted.
And I would not own my perch
without her restless calculation
over stocks and bonds, her frugal ways
and squirreling of cash that fed us all
long after her tiny frame,
indomitable and twisted as gorse –
a widow forty years –
squeezed a last breath,
and let us go.

She sleeps in Ireland now, beside her captain,
buried where his mountains meet his sea,
the house in Scotland boarded up,
and the lake of all our childhoods
haunted by the hungry swans.

The Painted Chest

It's purple, my favourite colour still,
a girl's petite bureau. He found it,
secondhand, and made it over.
I hoard it now, it is the last thing I see
before lights out, the black cat's silhouette
bids me goodnight;
the tulips and slender daffodils
wave me off to dreams.

He painted it alone, in the old house
after we had left, taken by my mother,
in her flight to a new urban life.
He must have been perplexed
in long evenings by the fire,
wondering how he'd ended up
abandoned in the family place
he had committed to restore.

I like to think – now that I'm grown
with two small ones of my own –
he fashioned the chest with hope
it would remind me of the father
he still cared to be, although left behind
for five days out of seven,
and later taken up with a new wife.

He had skill – the soot and orange cats
crouch and prance convincingly,
in memory of their much-loved,
real-life models, when they prowled
and skitted round the farm.

Each time I look, the purple chest
becomes a life-raft to a vision
of good intentions rather than
what it really is: a cast off,
redecorated to please a sulky child,
transported to an ugly street,
seeking talismans of return.

Phoebe Runs

Phoebe runs through giant dappled trees,
where on a curved low branch I swayed my beechy steed.
She runs through yellow horns of daffodils I once plucked,
across peeping purples of violets. April, my father's birthday month,
and the Spring wind flares out her tangled flaxen hair.
She pauses once to look for rabbits in the bank,
scans the horizon for the brown legged mare,
then squats and digs in moss to find a tiny newt –
sleepy-eyed, delicate-tailed – curled beneath a stone.
She runs across the spongy tennis court – where, 90 years ago,
her namesake served in whites – to bring me sprays
of cherry; shiny celandine. We take them to my father's
resting place; pay our respects to the family plots.
She runs to the pond with its yellow flags and languid trees,
lambs scurrying suddenly
when the dogs splash in a barking frenzy.

How timeless this old place can be
in sunny weather: ghostly children
flitting the long grasses, from every generation.

How High a Tree Could Be

I dreamed my little cat came back,
running in her grace and glossy coat,
all full with fur for winter,
and fluffed out in excitement
from a dawn inspection of her territory.
She rushed in to the house;
to me, still sleepy in my bed,
ready for food, to share herself,
allow my hand stroke her head to tail-tip –
my little playful pull,
her mock annoyance, velvet ears
turned briefly down.

The garden holds her now,
her light self starved to bone.
The cherry died in its standing:
its branches lost their hold in grief for her.
The useless roots still show their ridges,
scored with years of sharpening
from her busy claws.

I'll never forget her first day out,
how she cried so loud in ecstasy
at how high a tree could be,
calling me, so I would see.

Above All This

He is a naked root
in a bed of spines.
This is how it has been
all the weeks since the diagnosis.
A polyp in the throat,
morphing from a stingless jellyfish
to a pinching crab.
His whole life suddenly
up for grabs.
He is taken into the hands
of those who will scorch him
with precision rays;
fitted for rounds
in what looks for all the world
like an iron maiden.
Cased in black,
there's nothing of him left
to taste the air
except two nostrils.
His teeth have a special guard.
He fears for his beard,
for the juicy secretions
of his inner mouth.
For his youth.

To outstare the dark,
he feeds on everything green,
until his very blood
is rich as grass;
until even his dreams
are emerald clean.

Above all this, he knows,
a polished sun –
warm; radiant –
waits for him.

Airport Journey

First I take his photograph:
a firm smile, a trendy bristled chin,
he seems brimming with relaxation.
He jokes that next time he's home
he will not look the same.
Then we plant an apple tree
in honour of our young son.
We dilly dally with loading up
for his two month stint of radiation,
as though it were an ordinary trip.

At the departure gate we wait and wave
long after he is gone, me saying again
he'll be back for a weekend soon.
'You like me the best?' asks my girl,
who would not kiss her dad goodbye.
She's had enough of death
her first three years and now suspects
her father might join that side.
Her brother – tufted hair and buckled shoes,
still figuring out his steps – is her great rival,
as precious as she is, he has the edge,
simply because of his tiny size.

I take them to the shiny airport loo,
we wash our hands and leave,
trailing through the chilling maze of cars,
to find our own familiar ailing craft.
Our chariot roars with a burnt exhaust,
the rain falls. The children sit, quiet, angelic,
through the whole long miserable Friday traffic.

After their bath, we snuggle in the bed.
The house is quiet, ravelling off the strain
of recent weeks: the shock and frets;
their father's efforts to change his diet.
His need for them to treat him just the same.
His cool coping skills to the fore,
his lapses, the unspoken fear.

Soon they sleep, the boy cuddled to my breast,
her clutching my hand to her fleecy chest.
She sucks milk from her bottle
like an orphan lamb. For once I let her sink
to dreams without the hated toothbrush.
I sit and listen to the wind rustle the eucalyptus.

The Darkness Between Us

Arriving home from Germany
his plane is late; his lowered head
deflates my need to celebrate.
On Saturday, the ordinary weekend feel
hovers, cruelly – not quite within our reach.
By nightfall I'm flattened with exhausted grief.

He finally slips in to bed –
thinner than I had noticed –
quietly sorry and amazed
that the small things he must do
take so long, like chewing
and swallowing his food;
and finally getting to work on his computer –
the staunch ally that won't co-operate
in Heidelberg – the few phone calls
he had to make, the extra long ritual
of easing the children to sleep – so excited
that he's home – our girl staying awake
for hours to hear one more story,
feel against her back his familiar heat.

Only now he begins to tell
the darkness between us
of what he's seen: the horrors of the Clinic,
where men in beds beside him have no jaw,
no tongue, yet with the surgeon's work
have managed a cunning hole
to sneak the cigarettes they crave,
that are killing them over and over again.
He says the worst is when the baby –
the same age as our son, tiny and bald –
is brought in, like the others, for his radiation.

In the kind shadows of our bed
I begin to glimpse the full dimensions
of the coffin ship that is his time abroad.
What use to him the waiting hours
to read and listen to the music he adores?

I covet those hours horribly,
deranged with lack of rest. But here's my harbour –
the place he has swum back to for a short respite,
from where tomorrow he must leave once more.

Wing

I found the wing today,
a red glint on the dusty floor.
Broken off, its loss put paid
to the plane games
he played with the children.
They loved that little toy,
how he made it swoop
from the top of the door.
Then the real plane came
and took him away.

'I'm worried about Daddy,'
says my serious-eyed girl.
'We'll go on a big plane,' I reply.
'We'll find Daddy soon.'
The phone rings, it's him,
lying in his hospital bed,
wanting to tell her 'goodnight'.
'At least he can still talk,' she says.

Fingering the red wing
I fret because I have forgotten
where it was I stored
the other parts
that will make it fly again.

One day they'll fit back together:
the plane, the toy, the game.

Heidelberg

We go out in the snow to the lights
of the crowded market, our daughter
sweeping past us on a carnival horse,
laughing in her purple furs;
my mother buys decorations made of straw;
then, to escape the freeze of a real winter,
we scurry to sample sauerkraut,
the children wolfing crunchy fries.

But back in his grim flat,
peeling off the coats, we cannot overlook
the leaking pipe, the awkward stove –
where my mother gathers all her skills
to cook something he can swallow –
our daughter's timidity on his bony knee,
the fever gathering in our small son's brow.

Only when infant grumbles have eased
to peaceful snores, and I've planned
at last to take our boy to the GP; then he
strips to show me his shrunken spine,
the shoulder bristling with a new cancer –
a mole gone amok – that must be taken off
tomorrow. A new clinic, a whole new set of fears.

Ravaged by the treatment for his throat,
he makes little fuss, just quietly tries
to drink a glass of water. I wonder, frantic,
about the germs that infest our son,
and if they'll fasten on his father's suffering frame.
While I fidget he slips away to bed,
headphones clamped on
for the music that keeps him sane.

I hold his pale fingers as he surrenders
with pained relief to sleep, his cranium –
still capped with determined hair –
tilted up to suck every last breath
from the stuffy air.

Back to Us

So soon he has dwindled,
light fading out of him,
yet his tall form intact;
he is hollow and stooping,
his face a loose fold,
neck burned and mouth
rearranging itself around
the desert of his throat.
Without a shirt, it is fearsome
to see how little of him remains,
the livid scar upon his back
a reminder of more that could
have been removed.
Everything on the edges fits too large –
his clothes, his hair, his very nose.

He is an explorer struck dumb
by extremity, unable to find a tongue
to speak what he has seen.

And yet he eats.
Days are fashioned around bread and cheese:
he is willing himself back to us,
piece by piece.

In the Aquarium

In the Aquarium, the stout carp
thrust out pink lips
and swivel smooth flanks
in their shallow pool.
The rays, with their bat-like sweep,
push sinister dark noses
out of the water, and Felix,
my three-year-old, shrieks.
We hover by the tiny cowfish,
horned and bovine
in her watery meadow;
then the family of seahorses,
with their slender, curling tails.
We flee the terrifying eels
but find serenity beside
the huge shark tank,
confetti-ed with zebra and wimplefish,
the long-nosed butterfly fish
on his lone up and down mission,
defying the circling silver predators,
satiated and bored.

The children gaze at sleepy crabs,
spiny crayfish, the gentle octopus
with her limpid eye, her purple tentacles
at play with a twisty ball
(but if another octopus was placed
in her small palace, she would eat him whole).
We chat to the minute boxfish
who, like us, is prone
to boredom if there is no new fun
in the plastic globe that is his world.

Somehow these swimmers lull
the place of horror where
my stomach sits,
trapped in its own enclosure,
with the new picture
the surgeon has given him.

At home the children look at pictures
of lionfish and cowfish and sharks,
urchins, pufferfish, the inky octopus.
They jump on me, their hot little bodies
pummelling and tickling;
we agree our favourite is the seahorse:
the Daddy carries his baby in a pouch,
keeping his sturdy yellow tail
hooked around a rock,
his bony, intelligent face slanting down,
modest and gracious to the last.

Watermelon Man

(1993)

You Meet Yourself

You can get lost in America,
disappear from one coast
to another, the little lake
of childhood left behind,
bobbing with mementoes:
faces, nicknames, one-winged penguins,
the whiff of the candy store.

Then your head surfaces
on the crowded ocean of the new place,
you're another pebble on its beach,
clacking coldly against your fellows
on the tidal rhythm of rush hour.

Try that same voyage out in Ireland,
and you'll find yourself tripping
on your own umbilical cord;
forge ahead with a beefy crawl
and you'll hit a memory
at every stroke:
the grey brothers on the tide
transform into your old schoolmate,
your third cousin,
your neighbour's mother;

the shop down the road
is still there, and when you enter
your nose is haunted by the smell
of sweety biscuits and sliced pan –
the same immortal couple run the place;
the penguin sits behind your cupboard door
waiting to come alive at your opening;
the scarfed women still huddle on street corners
in corn-careful crêpe boots,
the jigsaw slots back into a kind of pattern
and, as you walk, you meet yourself,
turning casually down the same street.

Achill

Red fuchsia bells
drip from wild hedges,
tiny yellow flowers
stud the brown turf,
and the inscrutable mountain
lights to green clarity
when the sun
puts a finger
on Achill.

Then the sea is a bath
of salty diamonds,
on its dimpled surface
crawl the dark caterpillar shapes
of oaring curraghs,
the beaches are white sand
and clean aquamarine
licks rocky teeth
smoothing to cream
on shingle.

A few hours and the sun's touch
becomes a claw
flailing city flesh
to a raw fever.

In the pub
the thin-skinned tourists
swagger at pool,
challenging the locals
in their clumsy sweaters,
the few wind-shaven men
who were deaf to the city's
siren song.
Nimble in their boats,
they now shuffle shyly
with their cues

and pot their own black.

Blind Colours

My eyes are in my fingertips:
I don't see black,
I feel a rich fuzz,
a sinking into fur,
and I hear my cat crooning,
feel her claws knead my flesh.

Yellow is loud first
and then soft, like a mother
calling her child,
or like the sun, hot on my skin,
then gentle at the day's end.

Puce is a sudden flush in my cheeks,
an ugly notion of exposure,
but crimson and vermilion
excite my lips,
and orange is a round temptation,
a juicy feast on my tongue.

Green settles me,
I feel smooth leaves
with their little hairs
like my own cheek;

white is empty and clean,
I sense the air whistle
in my mouth when I say it:
white, echoing
and lonely, white.

Blue is rich but cold:
there's a feel of endlessness
about it, like waves
which never stop;
but turquoise is mysterious
and languorous,
my mouth lets the word go

regretfully, and I think
of strange places,
exotic fragrances that I'll never know.

Grey is soft and wistful
like the quiet cry
of a tired animal;
brown is dependable
like the earth, which is soft
if I fall, smelling damp
and comforting, full of roots,
steadying things.

We Were Like Sisters Weren't We

I stifled in that room
on the edge of that double bed,
you in your red cotton gown
hugging the other edge.
Backs to each other
I could feel your burnished hair
warning me off, sparking on the pillow:
keep to your side!
Not that I was anxious to flail about,
my pudgy toe accidentally nudge
your cold huddled feet.
I was hot, I ripped off
my choking flowered flanellette gown,
pushed into my hand by our hostess, fussing.
It hissed to the ground and
I moved carefully, letting my flesh spread.
You were so far away,
yet I scarcely dared to turn over –
you might decide to turn at the same time;
then we would have to feign sleep face to face.
Because neither of us slept.
I sighed and rustled, so did you,
but it was too intimate
for the feints of words.
I itched and wriggled,
raw in my skin in that hot bed,
nervous of your red sprite body,
so slimly, ethereally there,
restless too, but not naked, not sweating.
I had thought nothing of our sharing
this bed, we were like sisters weren't we,
but I couldn't relax.
Barbed sisterhood, territorially alert,
anxious to avoid collision.
In the morning, gravel-eyed,
I heard your polite yawn,
quick nightgown-held hop out of bed
to the solitary relief of a hot bath.

At Queen Medb's Cairn

They buried you upright.
Your friendly thighs
and capacious bladder,
all your largesse of limb
now lost
under a windscored heap of stone
which sits, like a button,
on the upturned belly
of Knocknarea.

As we climb to pay tribute
the mossy slopes trickle
with a gushing generosity
like your juices
after love;

the hilly stream
has hewn its little way
through rock and earth
like a miniature
of your bladder's waterfall
that delved the land.

At the summit
I struggle out of layers
to bare my buttocks
in the airy howl;

squatting with
a hesitant squirt
on the grey cairn,
a worshipper at the shrine,
a hopeful apprentice
of your ancient mighty wave.

Harvest

A flung stick,
and the children
stamp on green gourds
in the long-stemmed grass,
scrabbling out conkers,
squatting with their hoard
in the briars,
fingers pith-sticky and blackberryish.

In the field
mother stoops to cut wheat:
white-eared and yellow-throated
sheaves to garnish
the waiting church.

Late evening:
the men rattle to town
with trailers of grain
wind on their knuckles;
'If the dry holds up,'
dusty caps are scratched,
'If the bank holds off,'
wallets in shiny pockets
rub empty lips together;
magpies dart at yellow stubble,
and the church bell
tongues a warning:

they stiffen,
remembering a neighbour
tinkering with his baler,
his small sons
leaping at the wheel
nudging the engine
to wake and bite:
one child ran
to drown his heartbeats
crouching in the ditch,

the other hollered home;
but there was time
only for dying,
father's blunt hands
plucking at breaths,
dry leaves hissing in the graveyard.

The men close memory's shutter
and tramp to flickering kitchens;
evening sucks the last light,
dogs yelp at cars
in a hysteria which no one checks;

tomorrow they will sing:
'All is safely gathered in.'

Butter

In the first glow
of my laying out
I am all smooth
and golden –
a rich taste
waiting to melt
on the right tongue.

Then the knives come.
Dipping and scavenging,
they seek an easier passage
for dry bread,
they nibble at my edges
and stab at my heart,
leaving me pockmarked;
smudged with crumbs.

My plundered parts
are gloated over, licked,
spread out thin
with careful scrapes,
or smeared in thick welts
by greedy takers.

My solid sunshine
creams down their throats
for the gentle swallow –
the ooze between the teeth.

Broken into oily bubbles
by the churning
of their innards,
I endure the slow journey
of reconstitution,
biding my time
as I fatten again
to choke their veins
and stop their blood.

Mexico: Images

Quetzlcoatl, quiet serpent
and swooping bird,
when the solstice light
feathers down the angle
of the temple of the sun
you flicker into life,
sinuous and hungry.

At the mouth of the Jaguar dwelling
an obsidian heart
is nudged into my hand
by laughing pedlars,
a little black heart,
momento of red living ones
ripped out centuries ago
in the middle of these sleeping stones:
children, virgins, young men
fluting a different tune
for every step of death,
one for every foster family,
for every last suck of breath.

In the village
the faces are sober
at our bare-legged show,
and when we move to the musique tropicale
hands snake around us
reaching for crotches.

They call us the ballerinas,
the women won't look at us,
ashamed for our foolishness,
we retreat between our men –
the crowd writhes around us –
the black heart pumps
against my goosefleshed breast.

Pattern

Pain arrives,
on the slightest pretext,
making her home
in my belly –
a monthly visit is not enough.

I can feel her
hauling her bags
and hanging up clothes
inside me; the screech
of a chairleg
as she sits down.

The walls of my abdomen
lean in on her,
trying to force her out,
but only puncture
on her knitting needles.

She is fashioning
the story of my discontent,
drawing together the strands
into a bilious pattern,

some day she will slip
the finished garment on
and leave;

I will wear
the suffocating sleeve
long after memory
has sloughed off the encrustations
of outrage and regret –

pain has left her pattern
in my gut.

Spider

I open my mouth
and out she crawls,
the spider who's been hiding
down the pipeline
of my gullet.
She comes hurrying
with long terrible legs.
She wants to build a trap.
She wants to bite deep,
leaving the mark
of a poisoned tooth.
She's been in the dark
too long, crowded
with the flushed down jetsam
of so many days.
Now she's out –
her black body
sharp against the light –
her purpose fails her.
She stays still, playing dead,
weighing up the options.
In the dark it was easy to nourish hate,
the crooked spaces
starved out forgiveness.
She looks at herself:
a furry body, delicate legs,
a mark like a shield on her back.
Then she feels it.
A strange, exciting push inside
to move, to find her place.
Marking her corner
she feels the rush of thread
spun by her humming innards
meet the air, sticky and silver.
Running against the breeze
she tacks her baseline
and settles to weaving,
touching the outflow
of her silent language.

Balancing Act

I stand between two trees
measuring the distances
just as in childhood
I stood between parents
bisecting their separation.
A tender of the scales
I heaped more on the emptier side –
frantic for balance.

Now with you
I am at the other end
of the see-saw,
countering your down with my up,
your young with my old,
a past master of vice versa,
a juggler handing torches,
burning my fingers to make a circle.

Night Music
(for Liam)

Lake water
juggles the moon's reflection
into shimmering spheres
breaking and dissolving
on the shore.

The night
offers its hesitant overture:
lap and ripple
at our feet,
on our shoulders
a slow leak
from the dark cups
of leaves.

The sky is printed
with white fans of cloud,
pierced
by a bird's quick
reedy cry.

The wind sighs and settles
in the brittle arms
of the trees;
and faintly
a dog's lone howl
touches the single reach
of our listening.

Then, with your whistle
you conjure silvery notes
from the hills;
from lake end
to lake end,
echoes ride
on the air:
magic bubbles
breaking
on the horizon.

Watermelon Man

(a painting by Rufino Tamayo)

Watermelon man,
your curved melonslice grin
is pink as your namesake,
your crazy bashed old hat,
hunched shoulder and arm gripping yourself
as though chuckling inwardly,
a watermelon chuckle
trickling out of you
like sweet sticky juice;
you curve the ends of my black and white day,
my day of bleary head and blowsy self-pity
into a sticky pink smile
at myself and the world;
for here we are, cosy in my room,
alone together, shadowed by my lamp,
the chimes chink in the gusts outside,
my churning head is slowing,
taking a breath, and your
big brown pink-nailed hand
reaches across to me
and touches my lonely skin,
nudges my goosepimple ribs,
and I'm beginning to feel pink
with grins slicing all over me;
I'm a seed, a fruit, a luscious thing
snuggling in darkness, sticky with watermelon dreams.

Underneath Our Skirts

Although a temple
to honour one man's voluntary death,
his ceaseless weep of blood,
the women cannot enter
if they bleed –
an old law.

As the bridal couple glides
down the aisle,
her white veil twitching,
I feel my pains.
A woman
bleeding in church,
I pray for time,
for slow motion.
Unprotected, I bleed,
I have no bandage,
my ache finds no relief.
My thorns
are high heels
and itchy stockings.
He, the imitator, bleeds on
in numb eternal effigy,
his lugubrious journey of martyrdom
rewarded with worship.

Tonight custom demands more blood:
sheets must be stained
with the crimson flowers
of a bride's ruptured garden.
Her martyrdom
will be silent knowledge
suffered in solitude.

As we leave the house
of the male bleeder,
I feel myself wet and seeping,
a shameful besmircher of this ceremony
of white linen

and creamy-petalled roses;
yet underneath our skirts
we are all bleeding,
silent and in pain,
we, the original
shedders of ourselves,
leak the guilt of knowledge
of the surfeit
of our embarrassing fertility
and power.

Moon

A thumbprint
of smudged milk;

a cheekbone
climbing over
your scarf of irregular blues;

a bruised knee
pressed and puckered
while you bend.

Moon,
you show pieces
of yourself,
even in your
full disc
I sense
the rest of you
is hiding
in the dark,
a big woman
shy of her size,
showing a bare shoulder
or a coy toenail,

sometimes a face
shadowed and demure,
or roundly flushed;
Venus
the gem
on your quiet finger,
pointing our gaze
away

The Unravelling

I baulk at you
and want you,
and sew up the gaps
knotting the thread,
throwing back the wind's challenge.

But you open me
softly
when I'm not looking:
a dry sponge fills with water
with hopes
which can never be wrung;
these passages have blind endings,
my bold blood will falter,
back to the stitching,

but you're there
at the end of my seam,
and the unravelling
begins again.

Ophelia

(after the painting by Millais)

I'm lying here
caught in the watery reeds
of sleep, but not yet drowned,
still trembling and moving,
conscious of myself struggling
after one thing or another.

Then there's the sound
of your heavy feet in my room,
your clumsy, tender solipsist's hand
which drags me gently by the hair
out of my half-won pool of slumber;

and I empty my eyes
to look through the watery darkness
at your pale round face,
floating incongruously in my night world,
wanting to be near me,
to pluck me from my own dreaming
into your dream,
the world you carry with you
even in the other, waking time.

My words are draggled,
nets pulling a heavy body,
and thoughts jerking into surface clarity
like hands slapping you hazily away.

Your face goes quiet before leaving me,
leaving both the dreams
torn and incomplete;
my sleep gone, I clutch at my cold limbs
and know that you clutch yours
in another room,
the broken leaves of our imaginings
swirling down the current,
and us on separate banks, shivering in the darkness.

Woman Solstice

On the longest day
head bursting with hidden thunder
I go to find icons.
I am bleeding
bruised red petals,
and thinking of old bones;
new cries.
The sheela-na-gigs
lie in a dank crypt
flanked by ogham stones
and carved shards,
tagged and crumbling.
The sheelas squat on shelves –
forgotten; defiant.
One opens her legs
in a glaze of red,
one mocks death
with a thick glare
and a thrusting tongue.
Another gives herself joy
with a finger
on her pleasure pulse.
Some are featureless,
breastless,
but all open knees
pulling wide labia
with large, insistent hands.

They dare the eye to recoil.

The longest day
throbs to an end
blue light fading slow;
as I watch the roll
of the moon's disc
behind gathering clouds,
I am lying on cool sheets
splay-thighed
and smiling.

Making Terms

In this new place
I have to make terms:
cupboard doors jab my head,
the table bites at my hip,
the wardrobe steps on my foot,
as we make our awkward dance
around the room.
My open window throws in
the elusive vowels of new voices –
they pass me by
like anonymous runners –
then, as I sip tea,
and breathe the new air
with more trust,
a song plunges in,
from the red wink of the stereo,
your face daubs the walls,
my green silk dressing-gown
tells me how you looked in it
that night; my clock bleats the hours
that we talked, delaying
until grey fish clouds nosed the dawn,
even my breasts turn traitor,
crying how your lips
said goodbye, and then goodbye,
lingering over each –

I duck between strange sheets
to darkness, a clean empty smell.

At the Spa

There's an old brown man
in black trunks
and a bruised hat;
he wades to his place
in a ripple of poplar leaves,
and the water's lips take him,
licking clean the lines.

His face opens out
like paper pulled smooth;
he adjusts the hat
to a jaunty peak,
his bare brown shoulders
straightening, leaning back.

Half a world away
a young brown man
angles at his blonde date
in the Marin jacuzzi;
piped water froths
on her taut thighs,
her hands perch on the edge,
her golden head well clear.

His flexed muscles glisten
as he foosters
at recalling the game; his prize
her bronze, motionless shoulders.
The chlorine-scented water
bleats a modulated serenade.

At Sárospatak
the brown man
drinks the shooting sulpher water
from a plastic cup.
A woman with a lapsed tummy
engages him:
he stands, hip rakish,
she grins, gap-toothed and easy –
the water slaps them gently
into life.

103

Autumn

The mountain lays out her red hair,
brown undercurls and limegreen tassles
scarlet-tipped and flaring.

She poses before a backdrop of pure lapis,
the jagged defiance of the Gothic castle
her stone tiara, its fluted shafts of window
sheer to her copper beech brows.

Stop and listen – the silence is her withheld breath,
she's watching the day fall like a dry gold leaf,
as the cowbells die on the waiting air,
and the liverspots grow on her poplar lemon skin;

as a woman sifts through fragrant apples,
only to find an acrid intruder
hiding beneath their plump cheeks,
bruised and sunken, like a toothless mouth.

The Potters' House

The potters move like shy dancers,
pouring tea into glossy cups,
serving crimson apples and slow jazz.
Terracotta vases and teapots
queue beside their warm kiln
like shivering women
waiting for the sauna.

Cats skitter in the garden,
following me to the outhouse
where I pee before an audience
of brindled fur and curious claws;
air is clammy on my skin,
wild ducks gather in dark fragments
on the hunched grey back of the river.

I open their door again,
this time to a waft of coconut,
a crackle from the red-rimmed stove
and comfortable twilight
beneath low ceilings.

The potters are quiet:
their agent clacks the gate,
his spider legs scuttle
into the nest of his car.
Theirs is a tenuous hold
on the underside of the leaf –

when I go a vase is put into my hands
dressed in paper folds,
like a child
wrapped against the wind.

Old Women's Summer

Old women are moving
up and down the town,
like plump nuthatches
they bend to salvage
the heads of sunflowers
thrown in corners like pitted skulls,
they sit beside
fat bags of seed,
their fallen mouths
mumble over husking,
black kerchiefs in the honey noon.

In the market
old women are selling
veined purple beans,
the spotted globes of eggs
and windfall pears,
they offer Othello grapes:
'Sweet as pure sugar,'
dark as their eyes
in a trellis of wrinkles.

In the graveyard
old women tend the last beds
of their errant husbands,
paths are strewn with chestnuts
bursting from the pith
of spiny green shells,
the undergrowth flames out
like the flick of red petticoats
as the women swing carefully
onto the black skeletons
of their bicycles,
hands rooted, faces up
to greet the white glove
of the new season.

Auschwitz

Auschwitz:
sounds like a mouth
empty of hope
falling
to the death hush.

It's that hush
which today's birds
can't sing through;
the tourist shuffle
remove.

The earth is replete
with your lost flesh.

In the prisons
you built for yourselves
lie the left behind things:
the toothless brushes,
loll-tongued children's boots
pots past their prime,
a room full of your suitcases –
locked hopes from the old life
left unopened.

You are never more present
than in these possessions
that ink the outline
of your lives:
the piles of cracked shoes
recall your naked limbs
in the pits –
your swathes of hair
fill a room –
they took everything of you,
saved it for us,
whose tears cannot deflect
the accusatory lenses
of your broken spectacles.

Börzsony Hills

Past the walled village,
rutted cobbles,
and yellow twin-spired church,
we nose into the hills
to traces of snow
on brown undergrowth.

Our feet hesitate
on unrouted ground,
raised branches in our path,
wine bells of Christmas roses
collared in frost.

Then there's a sudden break and run
of boar, snouts up,
trotters marking the path
as their hairy bodies
lurch past the skinny boles
of hill trees in winter.

Stilled and silenced,
we listen
until the last sound
is our breath
on the white air

FROM

Entering the Mare

(1997)

Strike

I will sit outside your door,
my body shrivelling.
Not a taste of food
will I put through my lips,
just the odd swallow of water
to keep my tongue in working order
should anyone pass and look,
and wish to know your fault.
Think of me as you sit inside
at your full table,
a glass of stout
and a plate of hot food before you.
I am starving
that the world will know your cruelty.
I sit here so they will see my wasting:
the dimming of my eye,
the closing of my ears.
As I fade, your injustice
begins to fall away
from my brittle back
like a rough cloak
I need no longer carry.
I am moving beyond pain.
But my story thrives
even when I can no longer tell it.
It lives in the mouths
of those who have heard and seen me.
They are going to give me
the biggest wake
the town has ever known.
They will gather at your door
and take my vigil.
But they will not starve.
They will feed on my blood,
my bones, the last morsels of my sweet flesh.
They will swell with my outrage.

Make no mistake:
they are waiting for you.

Hunger at Doolough

The black lake is full of skeletons,
from the hundreds who trod the famine walk,
knocked on the door of the big house,
and were turned away.

On their long trudge home,
the lake wind took them
in bone-flinging gusts,
tossing thin, weary limbs
into the water,
where they swallowed death.

Luncheon was still being served
in the big house;
the lake – a pool of dark calm –
was shimmering through
the tall windows.
The governors of the town
lapped it with their soup.

We drink it now:
the lake, the long green sides
of the valley, the flinty rock
and curling mists.
We drive the quiet road,
and fill up on tranquillity;
we bloat with the view,
thanking our luck
we are the only ones here,
and have it for ourselves.

A few old farmers
leave their raddled ewes
to waddle the slopes;
they have said their piece
to TV microphones:
'You can't eat scenery.'

That is why
they'll sell their stony stretch
to fill their bellies,
on the weekend spree
of a lifetime.

They'll feed
the hungry claw
of the strip-mining company,
come to scratch
for gold.

Gold and bones
are hidden
in the valley
of the black lake;

and even as we turn our faces
to a rare caress of sun,
we are not satisfied
by the panoramic meal,
rolling out its solitary hauteur:
the falls
is a thrust of white water
at our thirsty eyes,
the wild pink rhododendrons
and yellow flags
lure our appetite
with their clever garnishing,

but biting in and quaffing down,
we find only a bitter taste
of greed.

Neck

Between the wig
and the blue satin dress:
her neck.

She is borne in a tumbril:
the crowd licks its lips,
thinking of the blade.
She has been dreaming
of blood falling
in a warm stream
down her breasts;
now she feels the breeze
at the small hairs
of her nape.
She feels the slime
of spittle
on her lowered brow;
hears curses rise
in a clot
around her.
She looks up once:
the women's eyes
are hating hard,
the men's cheeks
are reddening
with drink and rage.

I will give my head
for my father's big house;
for my education;
for the unusual dishes
we ate at table.
I will give my head
to them
who had nothing;
who starved;
who crawled with vermin;
who stank of poverty.

She remembers
her parents' feuds
and lovers;
the painted parties;
her favourite horse.
She remembers running hungry
through large, dishevelled rooms,
afraid, her small feet
cold on the marble tiles,
her belly crying
for bread
in the lonely dawn,
her voice trained
into silence
as the mansion slept.

They will carry my head
in a basket
and set it upon a spike.
All night
they will tear
each other's clothes
in fear or lust,
and my head
will watch,
the blood
cooling
and congealing
on my white
neck

City of Bread

(Paris, November, 1995)

I followed a trail
in the city of bread
on a fresh Sunday:
people walking home
clutching baguettes,
red-nosed in the winter air,
ready to enjoy a feast.
I found the open stalls:
trays of oysters, shelves of camembert,
the boulangerie crammed with croissants,
decked with long loaves,
hot and fragrant.

This is the bread of life:
the journey to find and eat,
the air keen on the cheek,
the mouthful of bread
satisfies the morning.

In this city of bread,
they gave their blood
to feed me from a full oven.
They knew there is no sure thing,
except a fistful of bread
snug in the palm.
Without bread you are without sense
or saving, heads must roll,
and swords must pierce the heart,
until the nose is calmed
by the smell of a crust rising.

Life is held in the warm
crunch and flake
and melt of good bread,
rolled on the tongue,
the comfort in the swallow.

My life is bread.

New York City, 1947

You were ten years old,
on your first journey
to the gleaming fruit,
that was ripe
for eating then.

It was all excitement,
party shoes,
and you on your daddy's arm.
You were his princess,
for a few precious days,
staying at the Plaza,
breakfasting
with him alone,
before his business meetings.

It was Broadway lights,
Central Park
covered in Christmas snow,
shopping and malted shakes:
all those frostings
on the cake of childhood,
that you hoarded and inflated
in the dreary adult winters
of rural Ireland:
no central heating,
no maple syrup,
no movies;
just up at 6 o'clock,
to milk the cow
and churn the butter.

You offered me your icons
as a dream of childhood
I could never have,
so when I made my way
to the big apple,
I thrilled and shivered
on the huge, dirty streets,

I passed up and down
like a hypnotised tramp,
before the massive facade,
and immaculate doorman
of the Plaza.

It was my afternoon off,
and soon I'd be back
in the Brooklyn flat,
where no air conditioning
cut the humid meltdown;
where I was nanny, maid,
consumer of leftovers:

nibbling
at the still bright crumbs
of your childhood's
New York.

Shepherd Boy, Transylvania
(for Attila)

He fingers the stiff keys
of the old church organ,
making the music
of his life on the mountain:
the wind heaving
past his narrow hut,
the yawnwhine and bark
of the shaggy dogs,
the bells jigging
on the jostling throats
of his sheep.

His green eyes
shine through dusty air,
as he fills the space
with sound,
like a bucket
fills with milk.
He is gaining the top of the mountain,
the animals running before him,
the dogs urging,
his own steps quick and sure.

But then his playing falters,
like his bad leg
on rough ground.
His new friends herd him
out of the church,
and on to the next adventure
of this strange day together,
a day that has him scrubbed,
put in his best clothes
and driven to odd places.

His friends
stuff sweets in his pockets,
block the sting of the wind

with a bright blue anorak,
give his poor feet pride
in white hightopped sneakers.

They want more:
to take him from the rough rhythm
of his old life,
from the acrid mouth
of his father,
from the smell of wet wool
on his hands.

They will not hear
his wish to stay
for the black-toothed song
his wages give the old man,
for the clean silence
of the mountain air.

Their questions confuse him,
he would rather listen
to the tinkle of the girl's breast
when the wind pulls the silver ball
around her neck. He shuffles,
his eyes travelling groundwards
at her nearness.

Fingers descending to the wet grass
he pulls out a ripe windfall.
Leaning to gather the firm, fragrant shapes
in his chapped hands,
he finds at last a return
for his friends' impossible gifts.

His smile bursts when they stand silent
to chew his apples,
and he knows
the swollen wealth of giving,
and why
they have come to him.

Yearn On

I want you to feel
the unbearable lack of me.
I want your skin
to yearn for the soft lure of mine;
I want those hints of red
on your canvas
to deepen in passion for me:
carmine, burgundy.
I want you to keep
stubbing your toe
on the memory of me;
I want your head to be dizzy
and your stomach in a spin;
I want you to hear my voice
in your ear, to touch your face
imagining it is my hand.
I want your body to shiver and quiver
at the mere idea of mine.
I want you to feel as though
life after me is dull, and pointless,
and very, very aggravating;
that with me you were lifted
on a current you waited all your life to find,
and had despaired of finding,
as though you were wading
through a soggy swill of inanity and ugliness
every minute we are apart.
I want you to drive yourself crazy
with the fantasy of me,
and how we will meet again, against all odds,
and there will be tears and flowers,
and the vast relief of not I,
but us.
I am haunting your dreams,
conducting these fevers
from a distance,
a distance that leaves me weeping,
and storming,
and bereft.

Sweet Woman

He'll go
after he has dug
a big space out for himself.
But first, he likes
a bit of resistance:
it's a challenge.

When, eventually,
I cave in,
he tramples around
my heart, lungs, lights,
until he has
a good comfortable bed
made
in me.
Then he leaves.

Then I'm a leaking wreck,
ready to double over;
the wind rattles my guts.
That's when I curl around
the empty space,
that's when I nurse
the hollow.
I rock the hungry voice;
I feed her,
I sweeten her loss,
I block her crevices
with happy tastes.

When he comes back
I'm a round display
of treat-me-nice
sweetmeats;
there isn't a niche
in the packed shelves
of my ribs
for him to get
a toe back in.

Warm Hand, Cold Heart

I reached in
to the glowing spread
of your sun-tongued flesh,
to find your heart.
My fingers coaxed the door,
it opened slowly,
snagged in rinds of frost;
the white heart breath
streamed forth, to offer me
cold cuts, snowed in fruits,
all the fare you'd buried
in that frozen core.
Out came:
your mother's dish of bile;
the clotted cries you swallowed
as your father beat you down;
the waif wings
of the girls you loved,
because they made you strong;
the party dishes
your jaded palate left aside;
the arctic lens
of your hermit's
watchfulness.

Your warm hand
laid a table
of aromatic meat,
and good wine;
but your heart
fed me on hoarfrost,
the pitted shrink
of rime;

and now
the door is closed,
and I am left
with a bellyfull
of ice.

Making Shapes

What you need
is whalebone,
underwire,
and padding
to lift, squeeze,
and magnify:
to give you a shape.

We all know
there's no hope,
unless a man can feel
like he's holding
two ripe melons
in his hands,
or else be fooled
into the promise
of heavy fruit,
cleft, and up
for grabs.

The ideal choice
is the remould:
slash and stitch,
a bag of jaunty silicone
on either side,
and next year,
you'll be Mrs Right.

The year after that
you'll have scar tissue,
a burst balloon
inside you,
your glands marching
against the foreign matter,
your brain on fire –

and everyone telling you,
you knew
what you were doing.

Report

'Celibacy is the greatest pain of my vocation.'

The words come cleanly
from your kind, thin-lipped mouth.
I take notes,
feeling my skin heat,
avoiding your eyes.
This is only a morning in my routine,
but with your wide palms
you hold your whole life out to me,
to be shaped by the whim
of my angle.
Your face contracts
in memory of the search
that led you here;
while all I can think of
is your body,
meant for nakedness,
sitting across from me
in a white robe and a black hood.
A junior brother,
you are the youngest
among the grey-haired,
and I am the first woman
to explore the cloister.
My pen slides in my grip
as I walk the corridors,
thinking of your bed
which has known only
prayers and pain.
Coming here
to 'escape the emptiness
of worldly things,'
you found a greater hunger.
Now you hope for God
'in the afterlife',
and today
the sanctuary splinters
as our hands touch.

The Man with No Child

He dreams
of planting his seed,
and pulling out
the wet plum
of the new life,
when time comes ready
for harvest.
He feels the years
gathering in him,
crowding his heart,
thinning his bones.
He is father in every sense,
except that for which
his globes of genesis
were formed.
He nourishes the stripling,
the stray,
the chance unhappy stranger,
the disconsolate friend,
the neighbour's sick child,
the burdened and tainted earth.
He feels as though
he is the father
of his own parents.
They do not dissuade him.

As the seasons taunt him
with their busy parade
of regeneration;
he settles into solitude,
like an ageing tree
beside a holy well,
branches laden
with the pennants
of hope and expectation,
hung there by pilgrims
who have come to drink
the waters of the well.

They depart light, carefree;
he remains,
garlanded with their leavings,
father of their abandoned dreams,
supporting
what they could not carry.

In spring
he still feels
a vein rush:
tormented, he waits
by the secret mirror of the well,
and all that he can see
is the reflection
of his own thirst.

Spits

Small boys appear
in shiny, lollipop suits,
crew cuts and freckles.

They are too young
to be disarmed by womanhood –
I'm just another moving target
for the hail of blind words,
which land like poisoned spits
in the quiet waters
of my inner ear.

With sure-flared nostrils,
they are drawn
to the victim in my eyes.
They pull my bag,
grab the keys,
hijack my car,
and demand
a chauffered joyride.

Their hoarse shouts
explode the kind angel in my head.
I want to kill them.
I want to break their little legs
like wizened sticks,
and roast
their marble-sized testicles
on a spit.

But nobody can catch them,
even if they haven't got
a matted pony to lash
into the sunset.
They are a school
unto themselves, small fry,
swimming through the meshes
of the nets
that trawl for larger prey.

Their shoal operates as one,
the snatched bag
travels effortlessly
from hand to hand;
the car window
shatters
like broken teardrops,
on a medley
of tiny, kicking feet.

Gambler

Smoothing his black hair,
his loose legs thrown out,
he is dishevelled,
the way ash caves
around a central glow.
Out of his huge green eyes
tongues a reviving flame,
as he remembers living high,
when he took the four grand
his aunt gave him,
handed over half
to stall the courts
on his unpaid mortgage,
and stuffed the rest
in his underpants.
He lost it in a night.
The spill of fear,
then the cool column
of certainty,
growing in his spine;
the swagger, the fall,
the black pit –
then the redemption
of the new bet.

Now he keeps a job,
a wife and children.
His dark skin no longer beats
with the bloodsurges of chance.
Now he crushes the lustre
of a new success story,
before its dazzle
consumes his reason.

His extravagant eyelashes
sink with their heavy lids,
but behind the screen,
the green eyes
are blazing still.

Choosing Fiddles

(for Brendan Mulkere)

His chin leans down
to her gleaming hip,
his fingers settle
on her slim throat,
he smiles
into sounding her,
his fond eyes
resting
on her well-formed curves.

He has already tried –
and left aside –
the one with the short neck,
the one with the showy voice,
the one that would not sing.

Now he draws
the searing lilt and call
of her, the bronze delight
of polished wood;
the ready strings
beneath his stroke
and swoop
become a loosened flight
of feathered notes,

falling
pure and long,
turning back again
for the release
of his big,
searching hands.

Entering the Mare

She stamps and shivers,
her white coat vainly shrugging,
as the would-be chieftain
plunges in, burying deep
his puny, acrid man's seed,
between her fragrant haunches.

The Goddess lives
in her fine rearing head,
the pink stretch of her lips,
the wide, white-haired nostrils.
Her hoof
might have crippled him,
her tail
whipped out his arrogant eyes.
Instead she jerks clumsily,
trying to escape
the smell of his hand.

Later he swims
in the soup of her flesh,
sucking on her bones,
chewing the delicate morsels
of her hewn body.

He has entered the Goddess,
slain and swallowed her,
and now bathes in her waters –
a greedy, hairy, foetus.

Rising from her remains
in a surge of steam –
her stolen momentum –
he feels a singing
gallop through his veins:
a whinnying, mane-flung grace
rippling down his spine.

Riding off on the wings
of the divine Epona,
he lets loose his dogs
to growl over her skeletal remnants,
the bloody pickings
in the bottom of his ceremonial bath.

* *The inauguration of an Irish chieftain, as observed by*
Geraldus Cambrensis (Gerald of Wales) in the 12th century.

Macha's Curse

She knew why
he did it:
he was a small man
with nothing
to speak of,
so to give himself
a leg up,
he boasted
about her;
how she could beat
all comers
with her fleetness,
faster than any horse
in the royal stable.

After he gave away her scent,
the noses came sniffing
at her hem,
and the king decreed
she show her colours,
or show the world
her husband was a fool.

She was carrying his name –
the name of a simpleton
she rued the choosing of –
in her puffed out belly.
But the king would not wait
even for another month,
when she'd be lean again.

She went alone
to the track.
She saw her husband,
watching,
among the men
to whom he'd spilled
her secret.

She set her teeth,
knowing that the race
was all about
his reputation:
he had put his pride
like a crouching,
sharp-kneed rider
on her back,
urging her to win
for his sake,
even as she ached
with the tiny spurs,
pressing her
from within.

She took her place
between the horses,
a small woman
in a plain dress,
dodging the hooves
and jostling haunches.

The whip cracked:
her bones leapt.
Her jutting belly,
and bloated ankles,
her tired spine –
all disappeared
in the might of her stride.

She shook her dark hair,
opened wide her breath
in the sweet pounding
of the track;
she smelled the sweat
of the horses
as she passed them by,
it sang in her nostrils
of long fields
starred with clover,
of vaulted hedges
full of birds,
and tails frisking in the dusk.

And then it was all
behind her:
the mayhem
of the crowd,
the panting foam
on the horses' lips,
the dim world
of her husband's house.

She fell
on the finishing line,
and in a giant shiver
her body opened
to pour out
her twin young,
their damp new heads
flushed red
with the speed
of their mother's gait.

She lay, empty,
sticky in her blood;
the men
were quieting the horses,
the women
were tearing strips of cloth
to wrap her babies in.

She took the lifestore
of her placenta
and put it
between her teeth,
swallowing back something
of all she'd given.

A great curse
began to gather
out of the ravage
of her torn flesh,
and she let it grow
until her voice
was strong enough
to make it heard:

'I curse all you men
who forced me
out upon the track,
knowing my time
was near,
just wanting
to see me bested.
You'll never have
the winning strength
I had today.

'Whenever strangers come
to fight you
for your land,
you'll find yourselves
cast down by the pangs
of a woman
in her labour,
and then you'll know
what your bets and boasts
have done to me this day.'

Lasting nine days
and passing down
nine generations,
the curse came on them:
whenever they had most need
of strength,
they found themselves
laid low
by Macha's word,
all their gallop stopped
in the heave
of her scarred birthing.

She wrung them out
like dripping shirts,
and hung them up
to dry in flitters
on the cutting line
of her cantering curse.

Horse Sense

It took the Lord
six days
to make the world,
and it takes a mare
six days
to consider,
to shy,
to startle,
flirt and nibble;
to canter,
trot and gallop,
circle and snort,
to lift her tail
and lower her head,
to begin to savour
his scent
in her nostrils,
to feel alright
about rolling
in the dust
with crazy hooves
in front of him,
to bite
his velvet flank,
cast her eye
several times
over his fine head
and girth,
kick up her fetlocks
and let him chase.

But there's no time now
left for any lingering
over the act of creation.

She is led out and hobbled,
back legs spread wide,
a strange stallion
kicking, rearing
and starved
is set on her,
to rend her
like a hot poker,
in front of
the sniggering yard men.

It would never
be like this
if she had her way;

if she were free,
like the wild horses
in the mountains,
she would take six days
to organise her miracle,
following the Lord's example –

or maybe
he followed hers.

She Whale

Great creature
carrying her calf upon her back,
strands of mermaid hair
about her stupendous head,
what has she to fear
from tiny men?
If they fall from their vessel
she bears them up
to air, gently,
like her own young.
They are no bigger
than the flip of her tail,
and their language
is equally minute
in stature or range.
They have no song like hers
to saturate their element
with sophisticated sound.

Imagine her surprise
when a crowd of such herrings
in a floating box
shoots a harpoon
into her head:
the shock of the grenade,
the explosion of the thick darts
that pierce her inside out.
Death comes in
through tent-like lungs,
collapsing them at last,
sucking in water to end,
like a struck man would,
by drowning.
Her tail is lashed
to the ship – a trophy –
her body leaking blood,
and her calf is left,
rending the waves
with its terrible cries.

Display

In the centre of the page,
let's put a large photo
of the winning artist:
his long hair blown back,
his lips reaching to kiss
the woman he has dressed
in a fetching suit
of polka dot, to match
one of his huge tableaux.

Let's talk about his art,
how he cuts up dead cows
and puts their bodies
in formaldehyde, displaying
the severed parts
for our delectation.

Meanwhile, let's give
a small paragraph, no photo,
to the news that the earth's caul –
which allows us to breathe
without frying –
is now torn so wide
that two Europes could fit
in the rupture.

Perhaps soon
it will be our own burnt
and disfigured limbs,
that will float in the ether
of the stratosphere,
for the delectation
of flying saucers
and their wide-eyed passengers.

Changeling

'Are you Bridget Cleary, my wife, in the name of God?'
MICHAEL CLEARY, Tipperary, 1895

Another woman
grows inside me:
she curls her lip,
she talks back.
She uses my voice
for taunting,
to try and open his eye:
to see what's wrong.

He says I'm away
with the fairies,
he tells the neighbours
and they agree.
They sit in my kitchen,
goggle-eyed, waiting
for signs.
She won't give them
the satisfaction,
she says:
'Yes, Michael, I am away,
to the place
your mother used to go.'

I know, even as
I hear her say it,
I've pushed him too far,
lifted the skirt
on the thing
I'm not to name.
I'm weak enough –
though I'm wearing
my Sunday best,
never wanting them
to pity me –

I haven't much fight,
for all my rising words,
so when he flings me down
I can hardly say
my name, a lapse
that gives him the rope
to hang me;
the proof he needs
to show them
I'm a changeling.

That's when the fire
burns my face,
and they all watch him,
and I know I'm gone
and she's gone,
the woman
who came and did this
with my voice,
she's left me
a shell
to be torched,
my flesh crackling
in front
of my own hearth;

and him saying always
that I was gone,
I was away
with the fairies,
and putting
the hot flower
of the log
to my brow,
and all our neighbours
watching.

Magic Brushes

(for Phoebe Donovan)

I

Brooms and butterchurns,
aprons and tongs,
pitchforks and bonnets:
scrubbing brushes
and feather dusters
body forth
'spectral evidence'
used to blacken bones.

Martha Cory made mysterious ointments,
Sarah Dashton was a haggard burden,
Anne Hibbens displayed turbulent passions,
Elizabeth How practised the healing arts,
Mary Johnson was discontented with her chores,
Elizabeth Knapp had an apparent teat
in her private parts,
Elizabeth Proctor did the Devil's work,
Mary Sanford planned
to make merry on Christmas.

Iron shafts
stab through muslin nightgowns;
a broomstick
becomes a cross.

II

My great aunt,
had you lived
in the fantastic strait jacket
of that time,
you would have followed
the line to the flames.

I see you, dressed
in your stained painter's coat
and felt hat,
dragged before the bailiffs,
stripped to find the witch's mark,
your body shared around
like spoiled meat,
your house and garden
taken for the godfearing.

Instead,
your brush-strewn studio remains,
with its paints and potion bottles,
charms of driftwood and dried flowers,
canvases of copper brambles,
cow parsley and crab apples,
charcoal men in shirtsleeves
at the threshing.

I enter and breathe in
the evidence of magic,
astride the broomstick
of your memory.

Tenterhooks

(for the Wynne sisters, who ran Avoca Handweavers, c. 1927-1967)

My maiden cousins
were wearing thin,
like old, light-leached cloth,
when my child's footsteps
first approached
their shadowy house.
Blind Winnie
stooping over the tiny faces
of the primulas she bred –
her magenta offspring –
and smiling in the sun.

I loved the leaf and heather
alive in the wool they dyed:
woven and wet
and pegged on tenterhooks,
it was a gorgeous ribbon
down the hill,
for passengers on the Avoca train
to marvel over.

I am certain of a time
when they knew what it was
to be bright and ready,
hung in the heat of an afternoon,
waiting for the right man
to step off the train
and claim his billowing beauty.

But Em's love died in the war,
leaving her with a ring
and a black dress;
Winnie found her bloom
in rich earth,
the touch of petals;
Veronica
stole scraps of time

for her books and easel,
woven in the loom
of her sisters' choices.

The new-dyed cloth
is me now,
throwing out my colours
in the heat:
ochre, madder,
blackberry, fern;
a rainbow
suspended over
the summer grass,
my glory dusted
with the pollen
of hill flowers –
daisy, clover, buttercup –
waiting
in the warm breeze,
for the teazling
of my nap;

until the day's end
when I am rolled
up tight,
cut down to size,
the golden day
a short-lived fragrance
in my muted colours,
my folds dry
and brittling.

That's when I'll slip away,
take my sun-blinded eyes
to my garden,
and breed primulas alone;
my ears deaf
to the sound of trains,
insensible to the tread
of sometime visitors.

Stitching

(for my grandmother, Marjorie Troop)

I send my needle
through ravelled wool,
catching the loose ends
into a cross-hatched darn.
This is how your freckled hands
smoothed the worn spot
over the wooden mushroom.
Pigeon-breasted in your mustard dress,
you bent your head,
snicking in the needle tip,
your fingers light and careful,
as you impressed upon me
the importance
of learning how to sew.
Your favourite backdrop:
a soprano soaring from the gramophone,
the sun sweeping in from the garden,
flouncing yellow swathes over your shoulder.
I have the quilt you made –
my limbs are lapped
in its glowing sunflower heads –
your last opus,
left for your daughter to finish,
and me to admire.

Tomorrow the quilt will be packed away,
part of the unpicking
of the home I stitched together.
I will wander the empty rooms
like you,
when your darning days were done,
and you woke up
in a strange place,
surrounded by strangers,

pulled apart,
the gap too wide
for mending

Grooming
(for my mother)

Dreamy and docile you sit,
as I comb out
the long ends of your hair.
Like mine, it is thin and straight –
a hairdresser's nightmare.

I have played with your hair
since I was scarcely
tall enough
to reach your reclining shoulder.
My small hands,
busy with their child's work,
seemed to comfort you.

Now you sit, slackly,
sighing as I pat and snip;
the brown swatches fall,
veined with grey: a splash
of last year's growing months.
Your face is delicate and girlish
as I guide the angles of your head.
My palms push you into reverie,
my pulls and swipes,
my amateur measurings,
my fussy trim.

It is a clumsy job.
Yet, as always, you shake yourself,
toss out the flattened strands,
and pronounce yourself glad.

Regretfully, you rise,
and go to sweep
the chopped grey-brown fluff
of your shorn locks,
as though cleaning out
the cluttered bedding
of a staled nest.

Totem
(for Catherine Church)

Out of the tide
of generations,
your cheekbones resurface
in my face,
your eyes slant mine
into blue almonds.
I have your Christian name,
and an old photograph
where your sepia mouth
closes in a prim
half-smile, half-rebuke.
Your long hair –
which I fondly think of
as a dark river
down your back –
is pulled tight
with severe Victorian pins,
your high, plain collar
stiffening your chin.
He has a kind face,
the blonde whiskery man
who married you:
your conversion
made you half-respectable,
malleable in your apology
for your savage blood.

Where did the tribal sap go
when you found
the stern father-God
and a white husband?
Did it rage
in your whalebone corset,
kick in your belly
like an overdue birth?

I imagine your torn days
shrugging off the Iroquois fears

of your husband's circle,
setting your face
against the clan mothers
and moon visions;
keeping your eyes fixed
on the stark body
of a milk-limbed man,
hanging from a cross;
your dreams flooding
with the heads of wolves
and beavers, the shiver
of the earth
beneath the thunder lunge
of buffalo.

This was your freedom:
a half-life,
yet perhaps you could see
the dwindling path
of your people,
now leading to a lost reservation
pumped with quick cash,
souvenir shops
with their heart-breaking canvases
of winging birds,
the numb bodies of your men,
out of their heads
with drink,
so that when the white car
runs over their legs,
they don't wake, or feel,
they lie bloating in the ditch
waiting for the end.

Is this what you saw
when you changed your name,
and squeezed
the wide, high arches
of your feet –
which I have inherited –
into shoes which never
fully fit, and will not
fit me now?

Blossom Time

(Tokyo, April 1995)

Crown of blood–orange,
and the sun comes up electric,
shearing off the woolly cloud;

a procession of brides
is floating down the hill,
arms held out,
heads held high
with veils of pale pink,
and trimmings
of wakening birds.

All day the pilgrims gather
to pay homage; all day
the brides pose,
delicate in their finery.
I wander beneath
their rapturous milk rose sprays,
confetti of petal
softening in my hair.

Dusk comes, bruise-coloured,
and the nymphs
take up their night poses
beneath my window,
fists of flowers
holding off the rain.

They pinken my dreams
with cherry lace and sap,
underskirt of leaf;

morning finds my plodding body
fragrant and aflutter,
and I come up molten
with the sun.

The Devil in the House

Floating on wingtips,
I halo the street
with my sugar icing smile;
get me home,
and I'll scorch your hair off
with my devil's breath.

Out of my satin pumps
my hooves clatter up the stairs,
off come the flesh-cramping clothes,
and out pouts my belly,
growling with relief.

How carefully I inspect,
and brush and scour
my poor unready self
to spill like new milk
out into the street
and light up your life,
my cheery white hand extended,
my tireless ability
to lay down my tunic
over your dirty puddles.

Now I'm home,
fangs unleashed,
I'm ready to bite
the hand that feeds me,
grub around in the filth
of my dwelling,
curse the day
I ever had to share this earth
with any living soul:
devil-happy, horny-clawed,
my wings hung up
for the night.

Gobnait's Shrine

The pilgrims are paying rounds
to Gobnait:
their lips
murmur over her grave,
their feet
scuffle past her church.
They bring their hopes to her well,
tie scraps of cloth to her tree,
slide their handkerchiefs
across her mighty bowl.
Standing on her sill,
they reach
to the sheela-na-gig
who dances over Gobnait's window:
pilgrim fingers touch her
with sudden intimacy, bare arms
reaching up through the narrow arch
to caress the stone sheela,
whose happy centre is worn away
with rubbing.

I watch the man's forearm
and reaching hand,
and feel myself
firmly grasped, my own parts
reverentially fondled, praised;
the overture of a dance inside:
Gobnait is whirring in the foxgloves,
the fragrant grasses,
the moving stream.
I drink from her waters,
taste her in my mouth:
her rising white trout;
her nine deer;
her magical bees
– whose avenging stings
drove away cattle thieves –
her agate bowl
that razed the invader's castle;

the sorry head of the man
who stole her horse,
and was hung after.

Gobnait, my heart is toasted
in your kitchen;
in you I find a place
I felt I could not claim,
where I can reach my hand,
dip my cup, hum
my own incantation.

Day of the Dead

(2002)

Day of the Dead, New Orleans

(for Lar Cassidy)

You would have loved one last night
of the syncopated 'Funky Butt',
with Big Al rolling
his great, luscious voice
out of the massive black mountain
of his chest,
the boys lifting their silver trumpets,
the flush in their cheeks
going right up to their thinning hair,
while the tomcat on the piano
sends his hands a-jitter
for the 'Charleston Rag',
and the sweet molasses drummer
drops his long lashes
and shimmies his cymbal.

All the vaults in the graveyard
are rollicking their brollies
with the beat and swish,
twirl and flourish;
in the voodoo haunt on Bourbon Street,
the obeah woman's hair stands up
with the tongues of serpents,
the clay ladies open their legs
and little heads peek out;
even Christ on his crucifix
has all the time in the world
for dixie.

My tears roll
when I think of the freezing day
we tried to warm
with our drums and poetry,
when we laid you down,
and carried your jazzy hat away.

In this city
where your shadow
takes a closer walk,
grief brims
like the upside-down grin
of the Mississippi
with its sad, booming boats,
and I think of you
as a great craft
powering down the current,

until your light failed
and you ran aground,
and we stood on the shore
in our Mardi Gras masks,
watching you sink,
wringing our hands;

and in your big marshmallow
and sweet-potato voice you said:
'Laissez le bontemps roulez,
laissez le bontemps roulez.'

Cherry
(for Phoebe)

You saw him waiting
at the foot of the bed.
He was fresh and young,
his brown eyes searching.
The tips of his fingers
were squared and bruised,
and you guessed
his trade was wood.

He told you of the splendour
of the cherry,
her limbs remembered
in the wardrobe's
sheen and grain;
even the shavings,
and the leftover crusts
of her bark
transform a hearth
with blossomed scent.

You offered him your hand:
delicate and long,
carrying in its lineaments
all the deft work
of your brush,
the fatigue of holding on,
when your heart
had lost its grip.

He took you then,
and freed your roots,
grown tired in the earth.

He lifted you
into the full flower
of the moon,
your feet trailing petals
like snow.

When I woke
for the first morning
into a world
where your breath
no longer stirred,
I wept into the empty basin
of my grief,

but now I smile,
because of your release,
into the forest
of the stars.

Bookey's Bridge, The Harrow, Wexford, 1798

(for John and Thomas Donovan)

You can speak of bridges,
of burning and hanging,
of building again,
and meeting in the centre
to shake hands.

I'd rather speak
of triangles,
of how I always cut myself
on the arrow-tip

pushing for closure.

Freedom, fraternity,
and godfearing
noble notions,
brought the cousins
with their cohorts,
bristling to the bridge,

John:
the cuckold yeoman
shouting for blood;
Tom:
the frightened rebel
choking him off;

right there
the yeoman's heart
shot out;
the rebel's heart
turned to stone.

The others ran away
from that family spilling,
lest its red triangle
soak the foolhardy motley
of their battle flags.

The Blood So Thin

Swathes of orange groves for sale,
the water garden grown over;
on the lake shore,
the alligators rise,
swishing their long tails.

You still dwell here,
with the ghost
of your movie star face,
remembering picnics and parties,
tennis on the lawn –
the score, love-all, a mockery –
your voice and clothes
a silken net of elegance,
your perfect hands
made for holding bowls of orchids.

The black maid serves dinner
through the shying lapses
of your conversation,
and I go to sleep dreaming
of the hourglass spider,
its poison tooth lurking
behind fragrant wood-panelling,
fattening
on the bones of your father
who made his own end.

In morning light,
I search the last
of your grandfather's estate –
the mossy groves, the rain tree –
seeking clues to his dark heart,
the fierce architect
of your drowned palace.

The heron's call
draws me back to the reedy shore,
and when on a sudden heel
of frustrated rage,
I turn away,
the beast makes a splashy lunge,
sawing up on waves
behind me –

and for one second
I feel the jaws
at my naked leg,
but when I look,
the ancient scales
have sunk to the mud,
and there's only a ripple,
a twitch in the water,
to suggest the snarl and bite,
the dragging off,
the appetite
that nurses itself
through decades,
and must rob from the sun
any heat it can get:

the blood so thin,
the teeth so long,
the grip
impossible to break,
if you let it
take you down.

Back on Smack

She's at the door, rattling,
and you clench, striving
for the strength to keep her out.
Your memory was of your bright,
fond boy, and the days when she
was his sweetheart. You forgot
that even then he was smoking it.
Since he died, she's gone on,
been married, her husband's now inside;
her children fostered out.
She's roaming now, feeding off
whoever takes her in.
She came to you –
her petal skin and big eyes
a reminder of the good times –
telling you she was ready
to pack it all in, just needed
a base to get herself steady.
It's been two weeks,
and she's stolen your cash,
your silver, your cards.
She goes out at night to score,
comes home in the wee hours,
waking you into fear.
Tonight's the last straw.
After she left, you put on the chain,
drank tea and smoked cigarettes –
you say eating makes you soft.

When the rattle comes
your dog bares her teeth,
willing you to keep out
the night thieves,
who have robbed you blind
and left you lonely,
with a packet of fags
and a bottle of gin –
and the house full
of pictures of him.

Song of the Half Breed

I was only half the man
her people wished for,
they suffered me
to please her.

I was bound
in the ropes of her hair:
she was fine-boned
as a fawn,
and trembling soft
in my arms.

She lifted me so high,
I had the strength
of a full-grown grizzly;
the spread of an eagle,
riding the wind.

After the white men
bled the best
of her tribe,
I led the way
to the cool grass
of the mountains,
where our young were born.

Full years, until the season
when I watched her
turn yellow and waxen.
The old women bathed her
like a doll.

I left our children
to seek the town –
all rough hewn wood
and fighting.
I don't know what
I thought I'd find there,
perhaps a sign

of my father's track,
but it was no different
from before:
shunning faces, refuge only
where the shadows
hid my looks.

A white woman
showed some kindness,
until her husband
came for me
with his drunken gang.

Now my crooked body
stiffens in the street.
Soon the tattered corpse
will be shovelled up
and buried, with the rest
of the town's cast-offs.

I wait, as always,
torn between two worlds,
hoping for one to come,
and claim my broken form.

In vain.

News Photograph, Grozny, January 1995

The little dolls are covered
with smears of jam and flour,
their mouths slack,
as though left down
in a gingerbread house,
by children,
baking.

Past the muzzy grains
of black and white,
I see
the dolls are children,
covered with smears
of blood and dust,
their mouths slack
with crying,
left down
in a shelled house,
by adults,
fighting.

The Bed

Today I strip the bed –
like pulling off a skin –
the bare mattress
is a quilted map
of places we never reached.

I twist out
the long screws
that bolt the frame together.
The bed falls apart –
a loose rack of bones.

It was a stormy night
when we first fetched up here,
you ferrying me and the furniture
to a last stop
before you flew off.

You fixed the bed together
so you could leave guilt-free,
knowing I had a place to sleep
among the chaos and debris.

Six years your handiwork
stayed put, me in it,
testing other loves,
or warming my own span.

After this dismantling
I feel like a prisoner
with the shackle off,

my flesh tender
from the familiar grip
I'd forgotten
I was wearing.

Coral

I buy you coral:
white, floral,
the one lure
in the giftshop
that shines pure.

Why did the coral
call me to its shelf?
It is all I want to be:
beautiful, unspoilt,
itself.

There's more:
its harsh pores – that sing
when your fingers lightly play –
suggest the hidden thing in me
that will not bend,
that cuts you
if you press too close,

and, if it's rattled,
breaks in jagged brittles,
waiting to needle you
in the dark.

Rival

Let me attempt to explain
how I aroused in you
such perfunctory passion:
there was someone else, who
was darker, closer, harder,
and opened up your dream
of fraught, forbidden ardour,
a cause you could believe in.
My body spread and waiting
was not the meal you craved,
you nibbled, fiddled, taking
with bored smugness what I gave,
and all the while your thoughts
were conjuring a scene,
where he was secret lover
and you were his glad queen.
His rough beard, your hairless skin
naked beneath his hands,
his sex, a heavy, rising fin
lifting you to different lands;
to the thrilling violence of his world
and the weapons he has hurled,
this handsome, grizzled, action man
is in your bed and in command.
He is your own lost other side
now stiff with lust and stiff with pride.
You open your eyes, but there's only me –
you're disappointed, naturally –
you wanted the press of manly thighs,
you'd swop my woman's mess of fruit
for the virile scent of gelignite,
you're getting hard at the thought of him,
but you're stuck with me, so you begin
to wriggle free, waxing maudlin.

Let's drop the farce,
I have no dart to strike your heart
and enter your sleek shapely arse.

Sunset

In the pink embrace
of the icy sunset,
the hills arching
their dark backs
to a last blue
and peach caress,
we marvelled
at the lingering
golden-tinged evening,
how it lit up the sea;
the red boats.

In that final
illumination
we let each other go,
our hearts sinking
like the exhausted sun,
after the orchestra
of light.

Island

I dreamed I was an island
of trees and spiderwebs,
and hummingbirds
trembling in my hair.

You found my shore
ready at last to say goodbye.
Our farewell was sleepysoft
and final, not the horror
of broken nights refiguring
our fractured past.

But knowing your laughing,
trickster ways,
I pushed you off
even as you kissed –
if I let you stay too long,
you'd quickly twist the throats
of all my little birds.

You did not press,
but when you left,
I found a scared
half-strangled body
in a tangle of my hair.
You had tried to pinch
one bird, and failed.

I took the panting creature
in my hand, and watched
the beak begin to calm,
the wings relax
their dull and frozen hunch.
The neck perked up,
the tiny claws had life again
to join the nesting flock
behind my ear.

Exhausted by your visit,
I rested in the crooning,
busying life of the birds,
the burgeoning leaves,
and spiders at their craft;

my spine and ribs
an oratory,
where my heart could grow.

Prayer of the Wanderer

(to Brigit)

Racoons shriek
and alligators creep
beneath my window.

Trees are lapped
by waterlog,
their arms bearded
with the tangled grey
of Spanish moss.

My hands
are wrinkled
and lost.

I wish for a mooncow
to carry me home
to the land of apples.

I would lure her
to my house
with sweet grass.
I would press my face
against her fragrant belly,
and try for milk.

I have left her sign
of woven rushes
over my door,
while I roam this place
of swamps and broken shells.

I pray she keeps all safe
till my return:

let my house not be fallen,
nor eaten in flame,
let my loved ones flourish,
and my garden thrive.

One glimpse
of the white star
on her great head
would give me peace.

Even her hoofprint
in the night sky
would tell of home.

Lost in Fjaerland

(Nesehaugen mountain, Sognefjord, Norway)

Blue crystals crown the valley,
spilling an apron of ice
with a subterranean churn
of glacier milk,
feeding the green sway
of the freezing fjord.

On the sheltered floor:
windless meadows of buttercup,
the hot smell of cattle
in the grass.

I'm halfway up the mountain,
air clean on the tongue,
a cuckoo in the pines,
rollmop of fern,
red lichen on grey stone,
the rush and sliver
of water melting down.

At the top – wrong-footed
by sudden drifts of resilient snow –
I'm lost, alone, surrounded by sun,
brilliant on white peaks:
an insect in a blind desert.

I squelch back without a path,
ears tuned for the gush
of the waterfall,
hands and legs scrubbed raw
by needles of dwarf scrub,
stymied by a sheer drop
of rock.

I am hours scrambling in footholds,
a wailing wreck stumbling
over rotting wood, scree,
sodden moss, clouts of snow,

heart-stopping steeps of granite.
Small clefts offer violets,
heathers, the delicate bells
of white flowers.
I fumble on:
sore, torn, bruised and wet,
dragging my fears behind me
like a skeleton.

Sounds of sheep bells
and wagging lambs give me joy,
their brown pellets
leading to something
that might be a path;

then, the breakthrough
when I find a shallow way
to a slope of sapling birch,
a sunny shelf, where I sink
into dry grass, my bones melting
out of the claw of cold,
watching a black spider
leg it through the blades;
above, a red squirrel
balancing on a branch.

The creatures mock me,
at home here, while I am at sea,
my eyes averted from walls of rock,
the chilly torrents crushing down,
the fields and tops of ice.

Skiing on Water

The silver surface of the bay
pinkens in the mountains'
folded rose,
the evening warm
as a loving cup
into which I fall
like a cartoon big foot,
my hands reaching
for the bar of the boat,
body crouched and braced
for the sudden pull,
the quiver in the knees,
then the miraculous
up;

water breaking
beneath my skim,
the motor song
of the boat pulling me on
in a zoom current,
through mountain and sunset,
over the sheen of the sea,
scudding and splashing
beneath my swoop.

I bend to the leap of spray,
then rise again
in the fleet throb,
hair flung back,
face split open
in a whoop of glee,

till the flight swooshes slow,
and I drop off
like a fattened bee,
helpless and heavy
from feeding on the wind,
shaking from the force
of what I have held.

Dip

Scuff down sandy steps,
arches stipple and sink
on crunchy damp stones;
shell rims.
Toes, naked pink
lead the wade,
skin gasping,
going down
into grey-green
thick of salt,
shiver of wave-tip
on thigh, belly,
breast,
up to the chin,
hair-ends
ribboning,
white arms
marked
with the cling
of magenta fronds.

Eyes rove
to whale hump
of mountain;
pink and yellow
of shore blossom;
the island
goldening up
out of the mirrorball bay.

My playbody
needs no virtual reality,
only this
late summer dip
in the sea.

Picnic

Green smell of crushed grass
as we sit and spread the food:
oily leaves of the vine,
fat beans' butter on the tongue,
crack of peppercorn; tart of olive,
the succulence of dates.

Late gold sun on our hair,
scented smears on our fingers,
and you full of memories
of gooseberries
in a boyhood garden.
Laughter rocks us in its chair
until I have to stop your mouth
with a kiss, savouring garlic;
almonds; the hum of wine.

How does the dizzy sandwich
find its way to the right place,
in the mortar and pestle
                    of our embrace?

About Face

Your face is a mask
of hazel and olive
in the secret valley
of Gleannta an Easig,
fastened on the dark lake,
the purple scree,
the frozen fall.
Yield of ochre needles
at our feet,
tongue of shore sand,
lick of lichen
on toothy rock;
and me
with the silent pines
at my back,
remembering
the intimate rafters
of your room,
my hands finding warm flesh
under black silk,
your face
spread out beneath me
full of smiles
like a cat
in the sun.

What Men Are For

You plunge the nap
of your otter's head
down the quiver and pool
of my flesh:

you come up gasping,
with pearls between your teeth.

Your face to my breast,
belly, thigh,
you coax me
to pour out my scent.

I plant my lips
in the toasty furrows
and ruby globes
of your beckoning form.

All night I am clasped
to the deep earth of your chest.

My morning hips are full of you
as I lurch through traffic
in a taxi to the train;

my mouth, red with kisses,
smiles in the knowing:

you have written my number
on your hand.

Him

He washes through my senses –
a lovely dye –
tinting me rose and peach,
tanging me pineapple,
like edible chunks of sun.

He stops the traffic
as he brings
my flowering wrist
to the press
of his lips;
his big boot
alongside
my lifting toes.

I quicken:
a burst of birds
on a blue sky.

He takes me
like a river
takes a stone;

or like the arrow
he flourishes and fits,

and lets
fly.

A Breath of the Rose

(Chapada dos Veadeiros, central Brazil)

Lovely Luciano
leads me safely across the river,
up the rain slip path
past the spines of giant palms,
and the fist-sized spider
lurking by my foot,
to the Valley of the Moon
where I glide in rocky saucers
of dark water.

At night he brings me
to the forest pool:
we bob in humming darkness,
the tufted tops of trees
and shyblur stars our canopy.

Lovely Luciano
has a voice like honey:
when he says my name
it sounds like cake.
He has tawny eyes
that watch and weigh,
and a slender nape.

In his heart
he bears a rose
for the music of an Irish girl
he has never seen: Dolores,
a name he lingers over,
savours.

Lovely Luciano
makes me lemongrass tea
when my stomach goes on fire.

He left the millions in the city –
the filthy air and traffic snarls
and taximen with guns.
Now he lives a simple life,
eating pumpkin as the crickets fiddle,
lazy in the portal,
so much left behind.

Portal

(Chapada dos Veadeiros, central Brazil)

Here are riches:
fat grass strewn with fairy glitter,
red dragonflies whisking in noon heat,
forest frogs serenading
our cradle loll
in the night of the hot spring.

Turbulent water pounds my flesh
in a head-drowning rush,
a pair of parrots haggle
in a clatter of red and blue feathers,
a green-tongued bootlace snake
circles in the apricot dust.

My toes splay on rock
to reach a ledge
beside a ton of water,
crashing on stone, spuming
rainbows down the gorge,
fern-lashed,
flashing with the metallic wings
of bird-sized butterflies.

Jasmine, mimosa, bougainvillaea –
my way is perfumed
with open-tongued blooms,
with the hot liquorice steam
of the hillside after rain.

I fly away
holding a keepsake from the garden –
a nest of clear quartz –
a drop spilled
from an upside down moon.

Abadiania, Brazil

Enthralled
in the vision
of what may come,
the pilgrims wait,
garbed in white,
for the man to incarnate,
for the bloodletting,
the stitching,
the miracle.

For long hours,
I hover
in the heavy element
of the waiting.
I try my shapes
to force a happening.
There's the fist
I wield in the water
that hits nothing.
There's the float
as I let go and hope
I'll be carried through.
There's the voice I find
when pain trips me,
and the lovely face of a woman
who outwits the stone
in her breast,
whittling it daily
with blades of light.

She glides through
the morass of people
to bring me succour.
She leads me face to face
with the wide eyes
of the man,
who sees and contains
misery; agony;
the despair of the dying.

I'm a voiceless squeak
before the big bear
sonorous force of him.

One look is enough
to sum me up,
before he turns away
into the restless field
of his vision,
the spreading map
of need and disease
in which I am a mere dot.

I go past a room
of abandoned crutches,
past the paralysed man
who is laughing
because he can move his hands,
past the little girl
who is still dumb.

I am as empty
as the blue balcony
as full
as the white oleander,

one hand
swipes numb tears,
the other
spreads folds
of my gauzy skirt
like a parachute,
readying
for the lift

Wow, João

He pulls through the tranced air
the hand of a volunteer
like a lion with a deer.
He flourishes his knife,
and scrapes the delicate gelatin
of the rolling eye.
He shoves surgical scissors
up the flared nostril
with a dextrous twist.
The head is pushed back,
gnarled and distorted
like a petrified tree.
In his grip, the scissors
delve and divine:
a miner sourcing gold.
A pull and flick,
and out they pop
in a fall of blood.

Spellbound,
the volunteer
is carried away,
borne in a chair
by swift-footed acolytes.
Blood from his nose
lies pooled on the floor.

The daze breaks
when the conjuror leaves,
taking his hypnotic hands
and regal face
to the wicker throne
in the white room.

We go into our lines
waiting for an audience,
we, the cautious ones
who do not wish for knives.

We ask him to work his art
with invisible stitches
and herbal potions;

to take our eyes
and gently tear away
the veil.

Visit

He'll come tonight
like a Milky Bar version of Dracula,
white cloak winging his big body
all the way from Brazil.

He'll find me sleeping,
arrayed in bridal white
for his delectation.
Like a little girl on Christmas Eve,
I'm hardly able to close my eyes,
thinking of it.

He's already had his way
with my inside,
and this is the last
of his ministrations:
to unpick the stitches
after my invisible operation.

I want to see him –
the big, red-eyed face;
the broad chest
and strength of him –
at his work.

But I'll be asleep,
dreaming of the room
where airy fingers
snipped and sewed
my scarred belly,
and I cradled myself in a thrall
of fascination and fear.

I'll be dreaming
of the long journey
when, weak and weeping
with queasy post-op blues,
I could scarcely lift
my baggage home.

When I wake tomorrow,
will I find a big handprint
on my lily-whites?
a telltale scalpel dropped?

I still crave
a smidgeon of the tangible:
he leaves me puzzling, mystified,
unable to explain
the change.

Confluence

Beneath the amber hood
of the street lamp,
beside the black gates
of the somnolent park,
we are eyed by fanlights,
flanked by motionless cars.

In this blind Georgian lane,
you lean in
to claim a kiss.

I offer you
my goodnight lips,
staying like a shut purse
in your embrace,
wary after years
of opening too fast,
my burns still hurt and proud.

Yet the sweetness of your mouth,
and your tongue – a luscious,
sinuous sea-creature –
is a feast I cannot resist;

nor can I pull back
from the strength in your arms
as you draw me close,
loosening your coat
to fold me
in your cinnamon heat.

Here it is, timeless,
a scene on a street:

a man and a woman
tongued and grooved
into one.

NOTES

11 Week Scan (34)
The Rotunda Hospital in Dublin offers a First Trimester Screening (scan and blood test) at 11 to 13 weeks, where the mother is told if there is a risk of fetal abnormality. After the age of 40 there is a much higher risk of conceiving a child with Down's syndrome. Abortion is illegal in the Republic of Ireland.

The Wave (47)
Robert Holohan was an eleven-year-old boy from Midleton, Co. Cork who disappeared in January 2005, shortly after the Asian Tsunami had wiped out thousands of lives. His body was subsequently found. He had been killed by a neighbour.

Above All This (71)
Written in collaboration with Orla de Brí, to appear with her sculpture, *Dreamscape*, at the Rhyme and Resin exhibition in the RHA, organised by Poetry Ireland in 2005.

At Queen Medb's Cairn (87)
Medb was the great warrior queen of Connacht. Her daring escapades and earthy, larger-than-life personality are to be found in Celtic literary and legend. She is a central figure in the *Táin*, the 8th-century Irish epic. Her stature is like that of a pagan fertility goddess. In the old tales, it was a compliment to a Celtic queen to make reference to her capacious bladder.

Mexico: Images (91)
Quetzlcoatl is a Mexican god, part serpent and part bird.

Woman Solstice (101)
The summer solstice was associated with female energy in pre-Christian Ireland. Sheela-na-gigs are medieval carvings of female figures exposing their genitals. They were carved on churches and castles (probably by stonemasons whose pagan beliefs were still strong) as protection against evil. Until recently they were considered too indecent to put on public display in the National Museum.

At the Spa (103)
Sárospatak is a small town in north-east Hungary where I lived for a year in 1987, when Hungary was still a communist country. The social scene at the outdoor hot springs there seemed very different from the hot tub scene I had witnessed in Marin country, a wealthy suburb of San Francisco, the previous year.

Old Women's Summer (106)
This is the popular term for autumn in Hungary.

Strike (110)
The hunger strike is an ancient form of protest in Ireland. In medieval times, it was enshrined in Irish law as a means of demanding redress. The aggrieved individual would sit outside the house of the offender, "fasting against" him. The hunger strike has been used as a powerful political weapon by groups as diverse as the Suffragettes and Republican prisoners in the North of Ireland during the Troubles.

Hunger at Doolough (111)
Six hundred people are said to have died in 1849, during the Great Famine in Ireland, at Doolough Valley near Louisburg in Co. Mayo, in the manner the poem describes. The area, which is very picturesque, is now a popular visiting place for tourists. During the 1990s it also became a focus of interest for gold prospectors.

Entering the Mare (131)
Epona is the Welsh horse goddess.

Macha's Curse (133)
Macha is the character in the *Táin* (see note on Medb) who puts a curse on the men of Ulster because of the reasons outlined in the poem. Possessed of supernatural powers in that she can outrun the king of Ulster's best horses even when eight months pregnant, she is clearly a personification of the horse goddess.

Changeling (141)
This poem owes its existence mostly to the research of folklorist Angela Bourke (in earlier times the writer Hubert Butler also highlighted this case) into the burning to death of Bridget Cleary in her own house by her husband Michael, who apparently believed the fairies had taken his wife and left a changeling in her place. It was believed at the time that if the suspect person was in fact a changeling, she would be unable to say her name three times.

Magic Brushes (143)
This poem was inspired by *Requiem*, an installation by artist Barbara Broughel depicting 42 people, mostly women, executed as witches in 17th-century America; also by the independent spirit and talent of my late great-aunt, the painter Phoebe Donovan.

Gobnait's Shrine (153)
Many fantastic deeds are attributed to St Gobnait, whose shrine is in Bally-vourney, Co. Cork. A sheela-na-gig (see note on 'Woman Solstice') is carved

above one of the windows on her church and when pilgrims pay their rounds on her pattern day (and on other days – pilgrims visit at any time of the year), part of the ritual is to rub the sheela.

Day of the Dead, New Orleans (156)
New Orleans is well known as the jazz capital of the world. It is also a melting pot of cultures and religions, from the Irish to the French and the African; from Christianity to Voodoo. Funerals there are looked upon as occasions for dancing and singing. '*Laissez le bontemps roulez*' is New Orleans-speak for 'Let the good times roll'. Lar Cassidy, arts administrator, jazz lover and pagan, had a New Orleans-style funeral and would have fitted into that city with gusto.

Bookey's Bridge (159)
This is a bridge at the Harrow, near Ferns, where the first confrontation of the 1798 Rebellion in Ireland took place, between a group of yeomen and rebels. The conflict was at its most intense in Wexford, where some families, such as my own, took opposing sides.

Song of the Half Breed (163)
My ancestry includes more than one Native Canadian forebear, on my mother's side (she is from Toronto). During supervised past life regression, I experienced the story told in the poem.

Prayer of the Wanderer (171)
Brigid is an Irish saint, originally a pagan goddess. She is the patron saint of poetry and protection (St Brigid crosses are woven out of rushes on February 1st, her pattern day, and put up over doors and windows – they are believed to protect houses from burning). Her emblems, such as cows and apples, are also associated with fertility.

Abadiania, Brazil (184)
João Teixeira de Faria is a psychic healer who holds court in a remote Brazilian village. Charging only a voluntary donation, he gives "invisible" operations and prescribes herbs. Without anaesthetic or sterilisation, he uses hypnosis, a scalpel and other instruments on volunteers with a variety of ailments, including cancerous tumours. The wounds heal quickly and painlessly. From impecunious locals to the wealthy who come from abroad, all who go to him seek a cure, but the results are not always predictable.

Visit (187)
A week after an invisible operation, the patient is instructed to wear white and lie on a white bed that night, as João will come to take the stitches out.